D0909052

SETTING NATIONAL PRIORITIES
The 1971 Budget

CHARLES L. SCHULTZE

with *Edward K. Hamilton and Allen Schick*

SETTING NATIONAL PRIORITIES
The 1971 Budget

713209

THE BROOKINGS INSTITUTION
Washington, D.C.

THE BROOKINGS INSTITUTION is an independent organization devoted to nonpartisan research, education, and publication in economics, government, foreign policy, and the social sciences generally. Its principal purposes are to aid in the development of sound public policies and to promote public understanding of issues of national importance.

The Institution was founded on December 8, 1927, to merge the activities of the Institute for Government Research, founded in 1916, the Institute of Economics, founded in 1922, and the Robert Brookings Graduate School of Economics and Government, founded in 1924.

The general administration of the Institution is the responsibility of a self-perpetuating Board of Trustees. The trustees are likewise charged with maintaining the independence of the staff and fostering the most favorable conditions for creative research and education. The immediate direction of the policies, program, and staff of the Institution is vested in the President, assisted by an advisory council chosen from the staff of the Institution.

In publishing a study, the Institution presents it as a competent treatment of a subject worthy of public consideration. The interpretations and conclusions in such publications are those of the author or authors and do not purport to represent the views of the other staff members, officers, or trustees of the Brookings Institution.

Foreword

EVEN THOUGH THE SPOTLIGHT of public attention and concern is today sharply focused on the issue of priorities in American society, the public is neither well informed nor much concerned about the composition—as opposed to the total size—of the budget of the federal government. This is a singular inconsistency, for the President's annual budget is the vehicle for the most important and comprehensive collection of priority decisions which our society makes in the course of a year.

The reasons for public inattention to the details of the budget are clear enough. The budget is not one document but four, ranging in size up to the 1,100-page budget appendix. It is highly complex, and it abounds with numbers whose meaning is often elusive. Although it reports the results of hard decisions among competing priorities, the budget does not indicate which choices were the most difficult or what plausible alternatives were available.

In this book three Brookings staff members, Charles L. Schultze, Edward K. Hamilton, and Allen Schick, seek to explain the 1971 federal budget as a set of decisions about national priorities made in the crucible of limited resources. They first examine the budget as a whole, its impact on the national economy, and its proposed allocation of funds among competing public programs. Specific programs are reviewed in an effort to identify the important decisions, to explain some of the considerations underlying them, and to survey the alternatives that might have been pursued. The book also examines several long-established federal programs which many observers believe may no longer be effectively serving the purposes for which they were originally intended. Finally, the authors project the "fiscal dividend" through 1975 under alternative assumptions as to major expenditure policies. The purpose of the authors is to explain the significance of the decisions reflected in the budget, not to judge them.

A number of scholars, both at Brookings and at other institutions, contributed background studies used by the authors in preparing this work. Their names, affiliations, and the subjects which they examined are as follows: William W. Kaufmann (Brookings), defense; Alice M. Rivlin (Brookings), and Robert W. Hartman (Brookings), health, education, and income maintenance; Henry Aaron (Brookings), housing and community development; Sar A. Levitan (Center for Manpower Studies), manpower; James R. Nelson (Amherst College), transportation; Michael F. Brewer (Resources for the Future), pollution control; John A. Schnittker (Kansas State University), farm price supports; Bruno W. Augenstein (The RAND Corporation), space; and John M. Deutch (Massachusetts Institute of Technology), research and development. Although the contributions of these specialists were essential to the preparation of the book, the authors are entirely responsible for its contents. Those who contributed background papers do not necessarily agree with the authors' treatment of their subjects.

Editorial assistance by the Brookings publications staff made it possible to publish this study ten weeks after the President's budget was released on February 2, 1970. John Yinger carried out the computer program used in projecting revenues and expenditures, and Nancy C. Wilson provided research assistance. To produce a volume with many tables and numerical references under a very tight schedule undoubtedly incurs the risk that errors may have crept into the numbers. That risk has been minimized by Evelyn P. Fisher, who supervised the checking of the manuscript in a very short time.

The views expressed in this book are those of the authors, and are not presented as the views of the trustees, officers, or other staff members of the Brookings Institution.

KERMIT GORDON
President

March 1970
Washington, D.C.

Contents

SETTING
NATIONAL
PRIORITIES
The 1971 Budget

Introduction

On FEBRUARY 2 President Nixon transmitted to the Congress his budget message for the fiscal year 1971, proposing federal spending of $200.8 billion and revenues of $202.1 billion. This budget, even more than most of its predecessors, reflects a series of very difficult choices:

- What should be the target for *overall economic growth* in the year ahead? What *mix of fiscal and monetary policy* is appropriate for reaching the target, and what surplus of revenues over expenditures is dictated by this choice?
- Given the expiration of the tax surcharge on June 30, 1970, an increase of 15 percent in social security benefits, and large, unavoidable increases in a number of other federal spending programs, how is the proposed *budgetary surplus* to be achieved? What emphasis should be placed on new tax measures as against expenditure restrictions as a means of gaining the surplus?
- What budgetary savings should be projected from *reduced force levels and combat operations* in Vietnam?
- What reductions are substantively warranted and politically feasible in *low priority programs*, both military and civilian?
- Even though expenditures are reduced, budgetary leeway remains quite limited. Yet the demands for program expansion in education, housing, pollution control, and a host of other areas continue to grow. What *priorities* should be used in choosing among those demands?
- Budgetary commitments in one year affect the budgets of future years. For example, appropriating $100 million in fiscal 1970 for nuclear reactors for an aircraft carrier implied later provision of $420 million for the carrier itself, some $410 million for the planes on its decks, $855 million for escort vessels, and $155 million a

3

year for operating costs. How will the choices made in the 1971 budget affect *budgetary leeway in the future?* What freedom of choice remains for program expansion in fiscal 1972 and the immediately following years?

The United States budget is not the document of an executive whose decisions are law, nor of a prime minister whose party must support him or bring down the government. It is, rather, a set of proposals to the Congress for action on appropriations and tax measures. Precisely because it must advocate the course recommended by the President, the budget cannot emphasize the difficulty of the choices made. It records the President's decisions, but it does not identify the close ones. Alternatives that were serious contenders for adoption but were finally rejected are seldom if ever mentioned. In some cases, programs generally recognized as ineffective or of low priority are debated but finally left unchanged because all participants in the debate realize how few are the lances a President can afford to break against politically impregnable targets. Thus, the budget is a document designed to persuade an independent Congress rather than to analyze policy alternatives.

The following pages seek to illuminate some of the President's budgetary choices for 1971. The study will (1) identify the major choices in fiscal policy and in specific expenditure programs; (2) consider some of the available alternatives and the reasoning behind the choices actually proposed; (3) discuss, by way of example, several federal programs that continue to be supported despite attempts by several administrations to alter or eliminate them; and (4) project to fiscal 1975 the revenue yield of existing tax laws and the expenditure consequences of current and proposed programs in order to estimate the likely size of the "fiscal dividend" over the next four years. The 1971 budget is the first in history to present longer-term projections. The projections offered in this study are spelled out in somewhat greater detail than those presented in the budget and include a range of alternatives that would depend on budgetary policies adopted in coming years.

The purpose of the study is to contribute to informed discussion of the budget, not to propose a different budget. It *examines* alternatives; it does not *recommend* alternatives. Its aim is to show the difficulty of making choices in a complex and uncertain world, not to criticize those who had to make them.

1. An Overview

In calendar 1969 a number of actions were taken that increased the problems of the President and his advisers as they struggled with the fiscal 1971 budget. Following the President's recommendations, the Congress reduced the 10 percent tax surcharge to 5 percent effective January 1, 1970, and allowed it to expire on June 30, 1970. The expiration of the surcharge absorbed much of the normal increase in federal revenues associated with economic growth. In addition, the Tax Reform Act of 1969, while causing no revenue loss in fiscal 1971, sharply reduced revenues for succeeding years and thereby inhibited new undertakings in the 1971 budget. And the passage of a 15 percent rise in social security benefits, rather than the 10 percent rise recommended by the President, added to the already large "built-in" increase in federal expenditures.

Constructing the 1971 Budget

The basic problem posed in putting together the fiscal 1971 budget is exhibited on the following page. Had 1969 tax rates been continued into 1971, some $210.8 billion of revenues would be forthcoming under the economic conditions forecast by the administration. The combination of reduced defense expenditures, resulting largely from troop withdrawals from Vietnam, and relatively uncontrollable increases in civilian programs, would have resulted in expenditures of $202.2 billion, leaving a potential surplus of $8.6 billion. Part of this surplus could have been retained for fiscal policy purposes, to combat inflation and promote easier monetary conditions. The remainder could have been used for some mixture of tax reduction and expansion of high priority domestic programs.

The 1971 Budget Problem and How It Was Handled

The Potential Surplus

Billions of dollars

- Revenues, if calculated for fiscal 1971 at 1969 tax rates (that is, not allowing for the expiration of the tax surcharge), would have been . .   210.8
- Expenditures, if calculated for fiscal 1971 only on the basis of a 10 percent social security benefit increase, a $5.2 billion military spending cut, and largely uncontrollable increases in civilian spending (including a federal pay raise on July 1, 1970), would have been 202.2
- Hence there would have been a potential *surplus* for program expansion, for tax cuts, or for fiscal policy purposes of **8.6**

How the Potential Surplus Became a Potential Deficit

- The expiration of the income tax surcharge will result in an estimated revenue loss of 10.8
- The extra 5 percent increase in social security benefits will cost an estimated 1.5
- The total loss of available funds from both these effects will thus be .   12.3
- A loss of $12.3 billion in available funds would transform the $8.6 billion potential *surplus* into a potential *deficit* of . . . .   **−3.7**

The Basic Problem Formulated

Even after a $5.2 billion cut in military spending and without any allowance for program expansion, the budget was threatened with a $3.7 billion deficit. Hence the basic problem became that of turning the deficit into a modest surplus and finding budgetary room for some program expansion to meet urgent needs.

How the Administration Handled the Problem

- Six ways were found to reduce expenditures by a total of 7.5
  They were: program reductions, $1.1 billion; postponement of the federal pay raise for six months, $1.2 billion; a reduction in the postal deficit, $0.9 billion; an additional net sale of government mortgages and loans, $2.7 billion; sale of stockpile assets and the Alaska Railroad, $0.8 billion; and transfer of cash royalties from the continental shelf oil escrow account to the Treasury, $0.8 billion.
- Three ways were found to increase revenues by a total of 2.1
  They were: accelerated tax collections, $1.2 billion; an increase in the social security tax wage base, $0.2 billion; and new user charges, $0.7 billion.
- The net effect was to increase available funds by a total of **9.6**

The $9.6 billion increase was used in two ways:

- The $3.7 billion potential deficit was converted into a $1.3 billion surplus; this required 5.0
- Existing programs were expanded and new programs were proposed; this required 4.6

The tax and social security actions taken in 1969 could have turned this $8.6 billion surplus into a deficit. Expiration of the surcharge will cost $10.8 billion in revenues in fiscal 1971. The extra 5 percent increase in social security will add $1.5 billion to the 1971 budget. These two factors alone produce a $12.3 billion swing, from a potential surplus of $8.6 billion to a potential deficit of $3.7 billion.

Thus, even after a $5.2 billion cut in military spending and before any allowance for program expansion, budget makers were faced with a possible deficit of $3.7 billion. The central problem therefore was twofold: to convert the deficit into the modest surplus the administration wanted for fiscal policy reasons, and to find additional resources for some expansion of domestic programs, including new initiatives. In the end, some $9.6 billion in budgetary leeway was found.

On the expenditure side of the budget, some $1.1 billion in program reductions were proposed, including a $400 million reduction in expenditures for the National Aeronautics and Space Administration (NASA). Many reductions suggested in prior budgets were repeated, affecting such programs as impacted school aid, the special milk program for school children, agricultural conservation payments, and a number of special veterans' subsidies. Additional new areas for program savings were also developed. The President proposed a six months' postponement of the 5¾ percent pay raise which, in other circumstances, would have been given to federal civilian and military employees on July 1, 1970, to keep their salaries comparable with those in private industry. This would save $1.2 billion in 1971 expenditures. Sales of strategic stockpile materials, amounting to $750 million, were planned. An increase in postal rates was also requested, estimated to reduce the postal deficit by $900 million.

Over and above these methods of reducing expenditures, a large volume of financial transactions was scheduled that would have the effect of reducing budget expenditure totals. The 1971 target for net sales of mortgages and loans held in government portfolios was set at $3.6 billion, an increase of $2.7 billion from 1970. Sales of these assets are netted against outlays for loan programs in the federal budget— the larger the sales, the smaller the budget outlays. Sale of the government-owned Alaska Railroad was estimated to produce $100 million. An additional $800 million was anticipated from a transfer to the Treasury of offshore oil revenues, now held in an escrow account pending the outcome of a legal dispute between the United States and

Louisiana over the ownership of oil deposits on the continental shelf. (A special master appointed by the Supreme Court has had the case before him for some time, and apparently the administration assumed that the dispute would shortly be settled in the federal government's favor.) Receipts from oil royalties are netted against the Interior Department's expenditures, and the $800 million transfer therefore serves to reduce net budget outlays.

On the revenue side, the administration decided to accelerate the collection of excise taxes and income taxes withheld by employers, yielding a one-time gain of $1.2 billion. It also proposed to increase the maximum wage against which payroll taxes are levied from $7,800 to $9,000, which would add another $200 million in 1971. An additional $653 million was sought through new or increased charges levied on users of federally subsidized transportation services.

Altogether, these actions produced $9.6 billion in expenditure reductions and revenue increases combined. That $9.6 billion was used in two ways: to convert the potential $3.7 billion deficit into a small $1.3 billion surplus and to provide $4.6 billion with which to expand domestic programs or inaugurate new ones.

About half of these actions, or $4.7 billion of the $9.6 billion, will have little economic effect. The increased sale of financial assets, while reducing the recorded level of federal expenditures, will not correspondingly affect economic activity. Without the added asset sales, the Treasury would have to borrow $2.7 billion more. But whether the funds are raised by sales of Treasury securities or by sales of mortgages in the federal government's portfolio makes little economic difference. Similarly, the $1.2 billion acceleration of tax collections means primarily that business rather than the Treasury will borrow in the market. And the transfer of the $800 million in cash from an escrow account to the Treasury will have no effect on government activity or on Treasury borrowing from the public.

To say this another way, there is virtually no economic significance in the difference between the projected $1.3 billion surplus and the $3.4 billion deficit that would exist were the financial transactions described in this section to be eliminated. But at the same time, the showing of a surplus in the unified budget was an important objective of the administration for psychological reasons. To have presented a deficit budget—even one that did not differ in economic effect from the surplus budget actually proposed—might have had a psychological impact on private market behavior out of all proportion to its true significance. Previous administrations, faced with the same problem, have similarly employed various financial transactions to reduce budget deficits.

The Economic Impact

The revenue estimates contained in the budget are based on a forecast of a $985 billion gross national product (GNP) in calendar 1970, an increase of $53 billion or 5.7 percent over last year. According to estimates implied in various parts of the report of the Council of Economic Advisers, this forecast assumes a 4.3 percent price rise and a 1.3 percent advance in real output. While the price rise projected for the year as a whole is still substantial, the Council of Economic Advisers expects the rate of increase to be considerably lower by the end of the year and foresees a continued slowing during calendar 1971 and 1972. The budget revenues projected for 1971 and the general discussion of the outlook in the economic report both indicate a resumption of sustained but modest growth in GNP starting in the second half of calendar 1970. This view of the near-term prospects is very near the median of private forecasts. There is wide agreement that growth in the first half of the year will be slow, although the degree of quickening thereafter is less certain. The division of the year's GNP gain between real output and inflation is also in line with other forecasts.

The $53 billion growth in GNP projected for 1970 is not only the official forecast but also the official target for how far the economy ought to advance this year. It is difficult to evaluate a target for economic policy at a time when the objectives of high employment and price stability conflict as they do today. In part the evaluation must be subjective, weighing basically incomparable costs of inflation and unemployment. In part it must depend on what else is being done to reduce the costs of inflation or unemployment to individuals. However, accepting our present arrangements and institutions, the target seems to strike a reasonable balance between the objectives of full employment and restoration of essential price stability. Any substantially faster advance in total spending would invite continued inflation at the present rate. For many reasons, there seems to be a clear social consensus that this is unacceptable. Any substantially slower advance in total spending would imply a recession and higher rates of unemployment, an unnecessarily drastic cure for our present inflation.

Accepting as reasonable the administration's target for 1970, how appropriate is the fiscal policy implied in the current budget? The unified budget, presented in the budget message and given the center of congressional attention, projects surpluses of $1.5 billion in fiscal 1970 and $1.3 billion in 1971. But for purposes of judging economic impact, the federal budget as shown in the national income accounts (NIA budget) is more relevant, particularly since it is not affected by such purely financial transactions as sales of financial assets.

The NIA budget shows a decline in the surplus from $3.6 billion in 1970 to $1.6 billion in 1971. This drop in the surplus does not, however, imply that the federal budget will become more expansionary (or less restrictive) in 1971. Rather, the decline is more than accounted for by the slowdown in the rate of economic growth projected for this year with its accompanying decline in corporate profits and increase in unemployment, which will reduce the growth in federal revenues. If there were no slowdown in the economy, the 1971 surplus would be $4 billion to $6 billion higher than the surplus shown in the budget. This "high employment" surplus would be moderately larger in 1971 than in 1970. In other words, the 1971 budget will provide somewhat more economic restraint than the current budget for 1970. This will be the case even if the Congress does not accept some of the measures proposed by the President to hold down expenditures. If past experience is any guide, the six-month postponement of the federal pay raise, the full $1.2 billion increase in postal rates, and some of the program reductions may not be forthcoming.

The decline in the actual surplus resulting from a slowdown in the economy does not imply a loosening of fiscal restraint. In view of the administration's decision not to return to voluntary wage-price restraints, the full burden of slowing inflation rests on a restriction of total demand by a combination of fiscal and monetary measures. In this context, a budget with a restrictive fiscal impact serves two aims of present economic policy. First, it contributes to restraining the growth of total demand or spending. Second, whatever the overall degree of restraint on total spending achieved by fiscal and monetary policy, a tighter fiscal policy, as reflected in a larger high employment surplus, permits an easier monetary policy with lower

interest rates than have prevailed in the recent past. The easier monetary policy made possible by fiscal restraint is particularly important
if housing construction is to recover from the current depressed levels.
Statements by the President and high-ranking economic officials
clearly indicate that the administration's fiscal policy is predicated
upon a desired easing in monetary policy.

Trends in Federal Expenditures during the 1960s

Table 1-1 provides a summary review of the major trends in federal
expenditures during the 1960s and serves as background for discussion
of specific changes in the 1971 budget.

In the first half of the decade, total federal expenditures grew quite
moderately, by only $5.2 billion a year. Defense outlays grew rapidly
in the first few years but soon leveled off. The remaining expenditure
increases were dominated by three elements: space, income maintenance (primarily increases in social security benefits), and physical
resources (chiefly highways and water resource projects).

Between 1965 and 1967 federal expenditures took a sharp jump,
growing by $20 billion a year. Vietnam war costs drove the defense
budget up at a rate of $10 billion a year, but civilian outlays also
began to rise rapidly. Compared to the prior five years, emphasis
switched from space and physical resource programs, whose growth
slowed sharply, to programs to meet social needs, which increased
very rapidly. The growth in income maintenance expenditures reflected the enactment of Medicare and Medicaid, while new programs
in elementary, secondary and higher education, health services, and
manpower training also led to large expenditure increases.

From 1967 to 1969 the overall rate of expenditure growth slowed,
as budget policy became more restrictive in an attempt to reduce
inflationary pressure. Defense budgets continued to rise, but at half
the rate of the prior two years. Civilian expenditures also grew less
rapidly. Almost all of the rise in civilian outlays was absorbed by the
growth of income maintenance expenditures; new social security
benefit increases were enacted, caseloads in public assistance programs expanded rapidly, and Medicare and Medicaid outlays continued to increase. After their initial burgeoning in the prior two
years, however, the newly enacted education, health, and manpower
programs expanded very little.

Table 1-1. Trends in Budget Outlays by Major Category, Fiscal Years 1960–71ᵃ

Billions of dollars

Category	Outlays					Average annual change in outlays			
	1960	1965	1967	1969	1971	1960–1965	1965–1967	1967–1969	1969–1971
National defense	46.0	49.9	70.6	81.4	75.3	0.8	10.3	5.4	−3.0
Space	0.4	5.1	5.4	4.2	3.4	0.9	0.1	−0.6	−0.4
Income mainte- nanceᵇ	24.5	34.2	43.9	56.8	72.7	1.9	4.9	6.5	7.9
Education, health, manpower	2.5	4.1	8.6	10.3	12.8	0.3	2.3	0.8	1.2
Housing and com- munity develop- mentᶜ	0.7	1.5	2.6	3.3	6.8	0.2	0.6	0.4	1.7
Physical resources	6.4	10.2	10.3	10.8	13.3	0.8	0.0	0.2	1.2
Interest	6.9	8.6	10.3	12.7	13.5	0.3	0.8	1.2	0.4
Other outlays (net)	4.9	5.9	7.8	6.2	8.3	0.2	1.0	−0.8	1.0
Sale of assets	−0.1	−1.1	−1.2	−1.1	−5.2ᵈ	−0.2	0	0	−2.0
Total	92.2	118.4	158.3	184.6	200.8	5.2	20.0	13.2	8.1
Total, nondefense, adjusted for asset sales	46.3	69.6	88.9	104.3	130.7	4.7	9.6	7.7	13.2
Annual percentage increase	...	...	...	...	...	*8.5*	*13.0*	*8.3*	*11.9*

Source: Authors' reclassification of data from *The Budget of the United States Government* for Fiscal Years 1962, 1967, 1969, and 1971. Figures are rounded and may not add to totals.

a. Individual categories are "grossed up" to exclude the effect of asset sales. Asset sales include: direct sales of mortgages and loans, stockpile sales, and (in 1971 only) realization of royalties from continental shelf oil escrow account. The 1971 pay raise has been allocated to each category.

b. Income maintenance is broadly defined to include the budget category "income security" *plus* Medicare, Medicaid, farm income supports, and veterans' compensation and pensions.

c. Includes rural housing and veterans' housing; excludes outlays for "maintenance of the mortgage market."

d. Includes $0.8 billion transferred from continental shelf oil escrow account.

The basic problem that began to develop in the 1967–69 period has continued through the present budget. Smaller outlays for Vietnam made possible a reduction in the defense budget; space outlays also declined. But increases in social security benefits, coupled with growth in caseloads and unit costs under the Medicare and Medicaid programs, will result in an estimated rise of $8 billion a year in income maintenance outlays between 1969 and 1971. After providing for a relatively modest expansion of funds for pollution control and housing, little room was left to provide for sizable increases in the education, manpower, and other health programs. At least for the immediate future, the largely uncontrollable increases in income maintenance programs, combined with periodic increases in social security benefits, will claim much of the normal growth in federal revenues. Barring changes in taxes or further sizable decreases in military spending, they will severely limit the possible expansion of other domestic programs.

Major Changes in the 1971 Budget

Table 1-2, which summarizes the principal shifts in outlays between 1970 and 1971, shows quite clearly how the composition of the budget will change. The overall budget rises by only 1½ percent, while total outlays are scheduled to rise by $2.9 billion. But this total is a net balance between $14.4 billion of increases and $11.5 billion of decreases. After eliminating the effect of asset sales and similar financial transactions, civilian outlays, apart from the space program, will rise by 11½ percent.

Looking first at the decreases, expenditures by the Department of Defense (including foreign military assistance) are estimated to decline by $5.2 billion. No separate estimate of Vietnam outlays is given in the budget, but it seems quite likely that the scheduled fall in military spending depends upon a continued reduction of U.S. involvement in Vietnam, both in troop levels and in combat operations. (See Chapter 2 for a review of the military budget.) Declining outlays for the lunar program, only partially offset by an increase in the new earth orbital program, will result in a $400 million reduction in expenditures on space exploration. As noted earlier, large increases in planned sales of mortgages, loans, and strategic stockpile materials, together with other financial transactions, will reduce the recorded total of budget expenditures by $4.3 billion in 1971. An increase in postal rates will be proposed to reduce the postal deficit by $900 million, and other proposed reductions and reforms will cut $600 million more from 1971 expenditures.

Of the $14.4 billion in budget increases, almost $10 billion is accounted for by programs that cannot be controlled through the budgetary process. Social security outlays will rise by $3.9 billion as a result of the normal growth in the number of beneficiaries and the 15 percent benefit increase enacted last year. Outlays for Medicare, Medicaid, public assistance, veterans' compensation, and similar in-

**Table 1-2. Major Changes in Budget Outlays from
Fiscal Year 1970 to Fiscal Year 1971**

Billions of dollars

MAJOR DECREASES from 1970 to 1971		
Department of Defense	−5.2	
Reduction in postal deficit	−0.9	
Asset sales and similar financial transactions	−4.3	
Reduction in space program	−0.4	
Other program reductions and reforms	−0.7	
Total decrease		**−11.5**
MAJOR INCREASES from 1970 to 1971		
Largely uncontrollable increases		
Social security	+3.9	
Medicare	+1.2	
Other insurance and retirement programs	+0.8	
Public assistance and Medicaid[a]	+1.0	
Federal pay raise	+1.2	
Outlays from prior contracts	+1.1	
Other uncontrollable changes, net	+0.6	
Subtotal		+9.8
Program increases		
Housing and community development (urban and rural)	+1.5	
Education, manpower, and health	+0.8	
Food stamps and nutrition	+0.6	
Water resources, excluding pollution control	+0.4	
Water pollution control	+0.2	
Airways, airports, and supersonic transport	+0.4	
Crime control	+0.3	
Other program increases, net	+0.3	
Less: Outlays from prior contracts included under uncontrollable increases	−1.1	
Subtotal		+3.4
New legislative programs		
Family assistance plan	+0.5	
Revenue sharing	+0.3	
Other new legislative programs	+0.4	
Subtotal		+1.2
Total increase		**+14.4**
NET CHANGE from 1970 to 1971		+2.9

Source: Estimated from data in *The Budget of the United States Government, Fiscal Year 1971* and *Special Analyses, Budget of the United States, Fiscal Year 1971.*

a. Increase for Medicaid calculated before the proposed $215 million program reduction, which is included above under major decreases.

come maintenance programs where benefit entitlement is stipulated by law, will rise by $3 billion in response to increases in the number of beneficiaries and, in the case of the medical programs, in hospital charges and physicians' fees. Even if the Congress accepts the President's recommendations, federal pay raises for military and civilian employees will cost $1.2 billion in 1971. Another $1.1 billion of increases will result from the payment in 1971 of contracts and obligations incurred in prior years.

While the President and his advisers had little choice but to budget for the $9.8 billion in relatively uncontrollable increases, the remaining $4.6 billion of increases represent specific decisions and priority judgments. Although the immediate consequences of these decisions can be seen in Table 1-2, their longer-run implications are not evident in the 1971 budget since in many cases expenditures in that year mark only small beginnings of larger programs.

Taking into account both short- and long-term implications, the 1971 budget appears to reflect the following choices:

1. A major initiative in the field of income maintenance. The new family assistance plan is budgeted for only $500 million in 1971, but even without further increases in individual benefits it will grow to an estimated $4.4 billion during the first full year of operation.

2. A housing program reflecting a somewhat smaller, but still ambitious, version of the housing goals enacted by the Congress in 1968. With respect to subsidized housing for low- and moderate-income families, the 1971 budget provides for a very large increase in rural areas; but, after a large jump in 1970, it makes no provision for a further increase in commitments for subsidized urban housing.

3. A rise in federal grants for water pollution control facilities to $1 billion a year, from a level of $200 million in 1969 and $800 million in 1970. The President has asked for a $4 billion appropriation to fund four years of this program in advance and for the establishment of a new financial institution to assist state and local governments in floating bonds to cover their share of the program costs.

4. A significant increase in the federal government's assistance to transportation. A five-year, $3.1 billion program of assistance to urban mass transportation is proposed. A new program of subsidies for the merchant marine will be undertaken, eventually adding $100 million or more a year to current subsidy programs. A stepup in federal investment in airways and airports is initiated, with added costs of about $300 million in 1971 and larger amounts in later years, covered by proposed user charges on commercial and general aviation.

5. The first increment ($300 million) of federal revenue-sharing with state and local governments. If enacted, this program is scheduled

to reach $5 billion a year by 1976 and then to rise more gradually in line with increases in the federal income tax base.

6. A decision, at least for the present, against additional large sums for the major education and health programs. Some small increases are provided for research and personnel training. In the case of the major support programs, principally assistance to elementary and secondary education, the budget reflects the view that too little is yet known about their effectiveness to justify large budgetary increases, while small increases add such a minute fraction to the education and health resources of state and local governments that they are not warranted.

In summary, the 1971 budget has the following major characteristics: (1) Through a combination of reduced Vietnam outlays, program reductions, and financial transactions, it provides for a $14 billion increase in civilian programs within a total budget that rises very little; (2) more than two-thirds of the rise in civilian outlays is required to cover continued sizable increases in uncontrollable outlays, principally in the income maintenance programs; (3) the remaining increase in expenditures is devoted to providing, in 1971, modest advances in rural housing, pollution control, transportation, welfare assistance, and revenue sharing, including the establishment of some programs that will grow significantly in future years; and (4) no major increases or new initiatives are devoted to broad support programs in the fields of education and health.

EVENTS SINCE EARLY FEBRUARY have led to actions that may eliminate the $1.3 billion surplus forecast for 1971. Wage negotiations with the postal workers will probably add to budgetary expenditures and increase the likelihood that the Congress will enact a pay raise for other federal employees effective on July 1, 1970, rather than January 1, 1971, as the President requested. The President recently released some of the construction funds he had frozen in 1969 as an anti-inflationary measure; he also proposed increases above the budget in certain elementary and secondary education programs. In existing circumstances, however, modest changes in the budget balance—including the appearance of a small deficit—would not themselves jeopardize the administration's basic economic objectives.

2. Defense

THE PRESIDENT RECOMMENDS that the nation spend $71.8 billion for defense in 1971, a reduction of more than $5 billion from the expenditure level of the previous year. This is a substantial and quite genuine cut in the resources allocated to defense. The reduction stems basically from the withdrawal of troops from Vietnam.

The 1971 defense budget is essentially a transitional budget. It does not yet reflect fundamental choices with respect to the strategic nuclear posture, the size, composition, and missions of the peacetime general purpose forces, or the relation between defense expenditures and the other programs in the federal budget. The transition will presumably lead to a new configuration of the major capabilities in the defense establishment, but the 1971 budget does not foretell how recent statements about strategy will affect force size and composition, and future budget levels.

The most widely discussed—but far from the largest element in the defense budget—are the *strategic nuclear forces* maintained to deter attacks by other nuclear powers. Two simultaneous developments have led to heated debate about the proper level of effort: (1) The Soviet Union has been decreasing the large lead earlier held by the United States in the ratio of deliverable warheads—although the imminent introduction of MIRVs (multiple independently-targetable reentry vehicles) could make the U.S. lead even larger than before; (2) both sides have acquired the technological capacity to produce significantly more effective offensive and defensive nuclear weapons. These developments have both led to and strongly influenced the attempt, symbolized by the Strategic Arms Limitation Talks (SALT) between the United States and the Soviet Union, to negotiate limits on strategic nuclear arms. Despite the understandable concern about

17

the competition, funds authorized for the U.S. strategic forces declined sharply during 1964–66 and, in terms of real purchasing power, stand at about the same level in 1971 as five years before. Taken altogether, the funds for the strategic forces and associated capabilities constitute less than one-third of the defense budget, as seen in Table 2-1.

The largest part of defense costs—including those resulting from operations in Vietnam—relate to *general purpose forces*, the conventional and tactical nuclear arms of the military establishment. This is where many of the less publicized choices must be made if a new peacetime configuration is to emerge. It is useful—both in highlighting the significance of these choices and in showing the implications of Vietnam policy—to identify separately the additional funds required to fight the war. (Note that this is an incremental definition of Vietnam costs; it measures the additional costs, not the costs of activities that would have been carried on anyway.) This too is presented in Table 2-1, which demonstrates the dependence of expected 1971 cost reductions on troop withdrawals.

The Policy Universe

The President's problem, in an area where units and equipment take years to develop and deploy, is to choose during a time of waning war a defense posture for a time of hoped-for peace. This requires criteria for determining the state of military readiness, nuclear and non-nuclear, that the nation should maintain in peacetime and during at least the initial stages of conflicts for which it is prudent to prepare. The resulting forces will not and should not be static; they will undergo modernization of weapons and other equipment, and they must possess sufficient flexibility to vary in size and composition with the capabilities of potential enemies. However, the criteria themselves must be sufficiently explicit in outlining the size, expected performance, composition, and derivation of the normal peacetime force so that it is possible to measure and evaluate change, whether stimulated by a buildup for a particular conflict or a shift in national priorities. Just as there is no perfect security, so there are no absolute defense requirements. Consequently the choice of a defense posture depends on weighing the military and diplomatic consequences of various

Table 2-1. Trends in Funds Authorized for Strategic and General Purpose Forces, Various Fiscal Years, 1962–71

Billions of current dollars

Authorization category	1962 Jan. 1961 estimate	1962 actual	1964	1968	1970	1971
Strategic nuclear forces	15.7	17.0	17.1	16.6	17.7	18.0
General purpose forces (other than additions for Vietnam)	29.2	33.2	34.5	37.5	41.7	43.3
Vietnam additions	...	...	...	23.0	17.0	11.0
Total	44.9	50.2	51.6	77.1	76.4	72.3

Sources: Totals are from the following U.S. Department of Defense releases: *Statement of Secretary of Defense Robert S. McNamara before the House Armed Services Committee on the Fiscal Year 1965–69 Defense Program and 1965 Defense Budget* (Jan. 27, 1964); *Statement of Secretary of Defense Robert S. McNamara before the Senate Armed Services Committee on the Fiscal Year 1969–73 Defense Program and 1969 Defense Budget* (Jan. 22, 1968); *Statement of Secretary of Defense Clark M. Clifford: The Fiscal Year 1970–74 Defense Program and 1970 Defense Budget* (Jan. 15, 1969); *Statement of Secretary of Defense Melvin R. Laird before a Joint Session of the Senate Armed Services Committee and the Senate Subcommittee on Department of Defense Appropriations on the Fiscal Year 1971 Defense Program and Budget* (Feb. 20, 1970). The costs of the strategic nuclear forces are an aggregate of the strategic forces program, half of the intelligence and communications program, 40 percent of the research and development program, and a varying percentage of the support programs (programs 7, 8, and 9). The costs of the general purpose forces are an aggregate of the general purpose forces program, half of the intelligence and communications program, the airlift and sealift program, the National Guard and Reserve forces program, 60 percent of the research and development program, the support of other nations program, and a varying percentage of the support programs. Vietnam additions are based on Tables 2-13, 2-15, and 2-4.

alternatives against costs, which in turn represent the other public and private goods we must give up.

The most convenient means to illustrate the choices involved is to determine the force configuration and budget level that obtained before the Vietnam war began significantly to affect the major budget elements, and then to examine possible changes in that *baseline force.* Table 2-8 on page 38 spells out the components of this baseline force, which in general terms included about 2.7 million military personnel, about 30,000 aircraft, and almost 900 commissioned ships. It encompassed nineteen and one-third active and nine high priority reserve Army and Marine Corps divisions, twenty-one tactical air wings, and fifteen attack carrier task forces. With respect to the strategic nuclear forces, the baseline budget was designed to provide an assured capability to inflict unacceptable damage in a second, retaliatory strike against the Soviet Union. In 1964 prices, this force cost about $51 billion a year. The $51 billion purchased not only the maintenance of the force, but also a continuing modernization of its equipment. The Defense Department has recently estimated that approximately the same force and pace of modernization (which in 1964, after adjustment for inflation, involved significantly higher expenditures on strategic nuclear forces than in any year since) would require about $64 billion at 1970 prices. Judging the adequacy of this concept of a baseline force, and developing alternatives, requires an examination of each of the major cost elements separately.

Alternative Policies: Strategic Nuclear Forces

Determination of the size and composition of the strategic nuclear forces depends quite critically on the relative weights assigned in the planning process to two objectives: (1) an assured destruction capability sufficient to deter a potential enemy—that is, the capacity, even after absorbing a well-designed first strike, to inflict unacceptable levels of human and economic damage on that enemy; and (2) a damage-limiting capability, or the means to limit the destructiveness of enemy attacks by some combination of offensive and defensive action. As spelled out in the following pages, the U.S. position in the past decade of significant nuclear competition may be characterized as an initial quest (in the early 1960s) for an assured destruction reserve and a second-strike damage-limiting capability vis-à-vis the Soviet Union. The subsequent deemphasis of damage-limiting capability occurred as the cost of providing it rose very sharply with the increase in Soviet missile strength. More recently there has been a resurgence of interest in damage limitation as mainland China moves closer to a long-range nuclear missile capability, and in the use of the antiballistic missile (ABM) to protect our missile sites as the Soviet Union develops greater offensive capacity to destroy those sites.

Throughout this period of increasingly obvious nuclear stalemate, the American concept of unacceptable damage to the Soviet Union by prompt blast and radiation effects has remained in the range of 20–25 percent of the population killed (around 50–60 million people) and 50–75 percent destruction of industrial capacity. However, the mix of delivery systems maintained to achieve assured destruction goals has changed markedly on both sides. The United States, which depended in 1960 almost exclusively on bombers and bomber defenses, relies in 1970 largely on hardened land-based missiles and mobile missiles at sea, although long-range bombers remain an important element of the force. The Soviet Union has achieved an even more remarkable transformation from medium-range bombers and missiles aimed at Europe to an ICBM force of launch vehicles that is already larger than our own, a submarine-based missile system, growing rapidly but still smaller than ours, and an antiballistic missile system around Moscow. These simultaneous metamorphoses have brought the two superpowers to—some would argue beyond—the threshold of a new phase in the strategic arms competition, symbolized in the United States by five possible new strategic weapons systems:

- the antiballistic missile (ABM);
- the multiple independently-targetable reentry vehicle (MIRV), which permits installation within a single missile of a number of warheads, each capable of being directed to a separate target;
- an advanced manned strategic aircraft (AMSA or the B-1), successor to the B-52;
- a new airborne warning and control system, probably with a modified F-106 interceptor (AWACS-F-106X), to intercept low-flying aircraft and those carrying long-range air-to-ground missiles; and
- a new underwater long-range missile system (ULMS) to carry much heavier and longer-range missiles than today's Polaris and Poseidon.

Research and development on all of these systems has been under way for some time. Deployment has been ordered for the MIRV and, on a limited basis, for the ABM. The evidence suggests that the USSR has long been working on an ABM and is interested in multiple warhead delivery systems. More significant to many observers is the fact that the Soviet Union has achieved a massive increase in the number of ICBMs, particularly the very large SS-9 variety which, if sufficient accuracy can be achieved, has a high probability of knocking out hardened missiles sites.

It is in this maelstrom of highly complex technological concerns and even more difficult questions of individual and social psychology that the strategic policy maker must operate. Moreover, in both countries his frame of reference must extend beyond domestic shores to the many countries that rely upon the United States or the Soviet Union for a nuclear umbrella and that have testified to their confidence by signing the Non-Proliferation Treaty. He must juggle costs and risks in a field where there is no longer any certainty that higher costs buy lower risks. Obviously, the range of choice is very wide and allows for substantial variations in the strategic posture. Nevertheless it is possible to discern at least three broad potential courses for strategic nuclear weapons policy. Table 2-2 shows the possible budgetary consequences of each. The cost of each option, measured in constant 1971 dollars, is assumed not to change over the next four

Table 2-2. Estimated Expenditures for Alternative Strategic Nuclear Forces, Fiscal Years 1971, 1973, and 1975[a]

Billions of current dollars

Alternative force	1971	1973	1975
Low budget	14.0	15.5	16.5
Pre-Vietnam	18.0	20.0	21.5
High damage-limitation	24.0	26.5	28.5

Source: The cost of the pre-Vietnam strategic forces is derived from the program budget in *The Budget of the United States Government, Fiscal Year 1971*, p. 84. Explanations for the low-budget and high damage-limitation variants are in the text.

a. The 1971 column shows the cost of each alternative in fiscal 1971 prices. In succeeding years the budgetary costs of each alternative rise, reflecting not a change in *real* outlays but an expected increase in wages, prices, and military retirement costs.

years. The increases shown in the table reflect solely changes in wages, prices, and military retirement costs.

First, one might settle on a configuration that accepts assured destruction capability as the proper safeguard against potential enemies but redefines its level of effectiveness to require fewer assured fatalities as the basis for deterrence. It would reject moderate damage limitation as self-defeating because of probable Soviet counteractions, and comprehensive damage limitation as impossible. Such a choice would reflect the belief that a restrained posture is most likely to lead to progress on arms limitation. This *low-budget alternative* would start from the proposition that, short of very improbable changes in the strategic balance that would enable one side to score a first-strike knockout blow, damage-limiting capabilities are not useful as military or diplomatic instruments and not worth the cost of major new systems in present circumstances. Such a posture would permit deferral of the deployment of ABMs (while continuing research), a stretchout of MIRV production and deployment, maintenance of AMSA and ULMS as low-priority research and development projects, and gradual elimination of much of the present air defense system while also holding AWACS to a research and development phase. U.S. strategic deterrent capabilities would then rest on a force of 1,054 perhaps vulnerable land-based ICBMs, 656 presently invulnerable submarine-based missiles, some of which might be carrying MIRVs, a fleet of over 300 heavy bombers, and a sophisticated command, control, and warning system. As Table 2-2 shows, resulting expenditures on strategic nuclear forces (and their share of intelligence, communications, research and development, and support) would be on the order of $14 billion a year in 1971 dollars. Adoption of this alternative would not preclude later review and policy changes, depending particularly on the future action of potential adversaries.

Second, one might choose an approximation to the *pre-Vietnam baseline* concept that emphasizes a rather generous capability for assured destruction, in a retaliatory strike, of 20–25 percent of the Soviet population, but admits of a need to develop damage-limiting capability against third parties and the requirement both to continue MIRV deployment and to start an ABM defense of land-based ICBM sites along with a thin area defense. This course would involve strategic costs on the order of $18 billion a year, of which around $4 billion would be available for a gradually phased procurement of at least some of the five systems discussed above.

Third, the United States could decide that assured destruction capability on the present scale is not enough—that high damage-limiting capability against both great and small nuclear powers is necessary to a credible deterrent, particularly from the standpoint of our foreign allies who, in the absence of such a deterrent, might be moved to build nuclear forces of their own. To reach such a decision, it would be necessary to conclude that the possibility of achieving the capability to limit damage to the United States to nominal levels is worth the risk of stimulating very large reciprocal expenditures by both superpowers, which could turn out in the end to increase the relative security of neither. If that judgment were made, the resulting defense program would provide for major expansion of three elements above the pre-Vietnam baseline force: more offensive forces, particularly sea-based missiles; a much heavier ABM and bomber defense network; and a large system for civil defense. The budgetary consequences of this *high damage-limitation strategy* are difficult to estimate, in part because so much would depend on the Soviet reaction. However, it is easy to imagine total expenditures for strategic nuclear forces on the order of $24 billion a year.

Alternative Policies: General Purpose Forces

Difficult and important as these choices of strategic capabilities are, their budgetary implications are smaller than those of the *general purpose forces* which exist very largely to protect our interests and commitments abroad. The two-thirds of the defense budget that reflects these forces supports most of the Army, all of the Marine Corps, all of the Navy except the Polaris fleet, and the tactical wings of the Air Force, as well as 60 percent of expenditures on research and development and a substantial share of intelligence, communications, and support costs. These are the military instruments available to support the alliances by which the United States is formally joined to forty-five countries—twenty-one in the Western Hemisphere, thirteen in Western Europe, two in Central Asia, six in Southeast Asia and the Pacific, and three in the Far East—and to protect American interests in other countries to which we are not formally allied.

Planning general purpose forces to deal with all the contingencies that may arise in such a broad geographic and political spectrum frequently encounters severe practical problems. Current analysis cannot precisely tailor forces to likely demand, nor is force planning designed to lock the resulting capabilities irreversibly into some fixed geographic allocation. Finally, the active and high priority reserve forces specified in such plans are not designed to fight a major war from start to finish, but to cope with the immediately available capabilities of the potential enemy while other reserves are activated and new units mobilized.

With these limitations in mind, it was determined in the 1960s that, taking into account allied forces, U.S. planning should provide the active and high priority reserve forces needed to wage the initial stages of major and simultaneous conflicts in Europe and Asia (as in the Second World War), and a sufficient capability to deal with a much smaller conflict involving U.S. forces in the Western Hemisphere at the same time. In Europe this meant that NATO should be capable of a non-nuclear forward defense against a major conventional attack by the Warsaw Pact on the basis of approximate equality in deployed combat manpower and tactical aircraft, in the rates of deployment of strategic reserves, and in the ability to sustain them. In Asia, the planning goal was the force required to withstand conventional attacks by North Korea or North Vietnam supported by mainland China. However, limitations imposed on Chinese forces by their deployments against Taiwan and the USSR and logistical difficulties suggested that it was not necessary to maintain equality in manpower as long as prevailing U.S. advantages in firepower, mobility, and logistical support prevailed. The requirements associated with the "brushfire" Western Hemisphere contingency involved only a slight enlargement of active forces (about one division, with associated airlift and sealift capacity). A combination of these broad propositions produced the pre-Vietnam baseline force sketched in Table 2-8 on page 38. The spectrum of possible force levels and patterns is as wide in the general purpose as it is in the strategic area, but again it is possible to describe three fundamentally different postures that would be reflected in significantly different budget levels. Table 2-3 provides aggregate estimates for these options.

Table 2-3. Estimated Expenditures for Alternative General Purpose Forces, Fiscal Years 1971, 1973, and 1975[a]

Billions of current dollars

Alternative force	1971	1973	1975
Low budget	34.0	37.5	40.5
Pre-Vietnam	44.0	48.5	52.0
Heavy modernization budget	53.0	58.5	62.5

Source: The cost of the pre-Vietnam general purpose baseline forces is derived from the program budget in *The Budget of the United States Government, Fiscal Year 1971*, p. 84. Explanation for the low budget and heavy modernization budget variants are in the text.

a. See note (a) to Table 2-2.

First is the possibility of shifting the broad planning assumption to allow for only one major conflict and one minor one at any one time—or shifting to a *low-budget general purpose force*. This suggestion is frequently based on the explicit or implicit proposition that, despite uncertainty in Vietnam and Laos and commitments in Thailand and the Republic of Korea, the United States need not prepare for another major land war in Asia. Alternatively, it is sometimes suggested that even though we could use a large part of the remaining single major-war capability to respond to an Asian contingency, the problem involved in so doing would exert a useful restraining influence on the President. If adopted, this posture might lead to elimination of as many as six Army divisions, three wings of tactical aircraft, and six attack carriers, along with a significant reduction in amphibious assault and anti-submarine warfare (ASW) forces in the Pacific. The resulting decline in expenditures would be at least $10 billion a year (at 1971 prices) below the pre-Vietnam baseline of $44 billion, to a level of about $34 billion a year; but it would leave the United States with two Marine divisions with air wings, at least one attack carrier on station, and four fighter/bomber wings available for service in the Pacific.

Second, the nation might elect to continue with the *pre-Vietnam baseline force*, which was intended to have the capability simultaneously to make an initial response in two major wars and one minor conflict. It also emphasized the mobility of U.S.-based men and equipment to permit both flexible geographic allocation and protection against the necessity to use nuclear weapons early in a conflict. This posture would express a willingness on the part of the United States to maintain its military readiness with respect to both Europe and Asia, or to engage in a very large-scale effort in one theater at a time. It would cost on the order of $44 billion a year at 1971 prices.

Third, it might be decided that the U.S. posture should be based on two major and one minor conflicts but that the forces in being should be substantially improved in firepower, mobility, tactical air support, and the like. The result might be called a *heavy modernization budget*. It would permit much greater tactical mobility and firepower for the land forces, large-scale acquisition of the F-14 and F-15 fighters, an increase in attack carrier task forces, more "high speed" attack submarines and ASW escorts, at least two more C-5A airlift squadrons for strategic mobility, and the increased outlays for operation and maintenance that would go with these advanced weapon systems. The cost of such a posture would be around $53 billion in 1971 prices.

Vietnam Costs

The discussion of policy alternatives to this point has concerned itself entirely with alternative peacetime defense postures. Obviously, the final element necessary to link these options and their budgetary consequences to the real world of the next few years is to estimate the future costs of the Vietnam conflict. There are no official projections of Vietnam force levels or budgetary costs beyond what one can infer from the President's announced intention to continue the troop withdrawals, which are scheduled to reach 115,500 by April 15, 1970. Table 2-4 shows a possible schedule of withdrawals and associated expenditure levels for illustrative purposes; it seems as reasonable as any and is incorporated below in the overall alternative estimates. This treatment also reflects the view that there is no substantial "deferred deficit" of equipment, supplies, or facilities that must be made up after the war ends, a conclusion for which the reasoning appears in the latter part of this chapter.

Table 2-4. Expenditure Levels for Illustrative Vietnam Disengagement Program, Fiscal Years 1969–75

Item	1969	1970	1971	1972	1973	1974	1975
Military personnel (thousands of men)	538	380	200	50	0	0	0
Incremental outlays (billions of dollars)	23	17	11	3	1.5	1	1

Note: These are purely illustrative estimates. However, through fiscal 1971 they are roughly consistent with the budget document projections of total armed forces personnel strength shown in Table 2-7. See also Tables 2-11, 2-13, and 2-15 for the cost calculations. All figures are as of the end of the fiscal year to which they relate.

The President must build his defense budget recommendations out of three major components: strategic nuclear forces, general purpose forces, and incremental forces for Vietnam. It used to be argued that the first two were inversely related, but recent thinking largely holds that deterrence of nuclear attack and readiness for conventional conflict are two quite different problems in which the capability for one is not much related to the capability for the other.

Thus the President has what amounts to a matrix of possibilities that provides at least nine different levels of defense spending. Table 2-5 shows these possibilities projected over five years, incorporating expected wage and price changes during the period. Each alternative also includes Vietnam estimates according to the above schedule. In 1971 prices the alternatives range from $59 billion to $88 billion; by 1975, taking account of reduced Vietnam costs on the one hand and higher prices and wages on the other, the range is from $58 billion to $92 billion. Again, it should be remembered that variation from these broad projections is not only possible but extremely likely. These figures are neither more nor less than orders of magnitude corresponding to the major options identified.

Thrust of the 1971 Budget

Table 2-6 breaks down the 1971 defense budget proposals by program. It highlights the fact that, despite the administration's policy to proceed with the Safeguard ABM and the testing and deployment of MIRVs, only a very moderate increase is proposed in funds authorized for strategic nuclear forces. In general, the $5 billion in expenditure cuts results from disengagement in Vietnam. The President's February message on U.S. foreign policy for the 1970s clearly indicates that a reexamination of U.S. military doctrine with respect to possible future engagement in a major land war in Asia has taken

Table 2-5. Five-Year Defense Budget Projections on Various Policy Assumptions Incorporating Vietnam Estimates, Fiscal Years 1971, 1973, and 1975[a]

Billions of current dollars

Assumptions[b]	1971	1973	1975
Low-budget SNF; Low-budget GPF	59	54½	58
Low-budget SNF; Pre-Vietnam GPF	69	65½	69½
Low-budget SNF; Heavy-modernization GPF	78	75½	80
Pre-Vietnam SNF; Low-budget GPF	63	59	63
Pre-Vietnam SNF; Pre-Vietnam GPF[c]	73	70	74½
Pre-Vietnam SNF; Heavy-modernization GPF	82	80	85
High damage-limitation SNF; Low-budget GPF	69	65½	70
High damage-limitation SNF; Pre-Vietnam GPF	79	76½	81½
High damage-limitation SNF; Heavy-modernization GPF	88	86½	92
Vietnam outlays included in each of the above	(11)	(1.5)	(1.0)

Source: Based on Tables 2-2 and 2-3, and on calculations shown in the text.
a. The costs of each alternative change between 1971 and later years for two reasons: rising wages and prices [see note (a) to Table 2-2], and declining outlays for the war in Vietnam.
b. SNF means strategic nuclear forces; GPF means general purpose forces.
c. This is the pre-Vietnam baseline force.

Table 2-6. Department of Defense Obligational Authority by Major Military Program, Fiscal Years 1969–71

Billions of current dollars

Program	1969 actual	1970 estimate	1971 estimate
Strategic forces	8.6	7.5	7.9
General purpose forces	30.7	27.8	24.7
Intelligence and communications	5.8	5.6	5.2
Airlift and sealift	1.6	1.7	1.5
National Guard and Reserve forces	2.1	2.5	2.5
Research and development	4.7	4.8	5.4
Central supply and maintenance	9.4	9.4	8.4
Training, medical, and other general personnel activities	12.4	13.0	12.6
Administration and associated activities	1.3	1.5	1.5
Support of other nations	2.2	2.4	2.5
Total	78.7	76.4	72.3
Composition of total:			
New budget authority	77.0	73.5	70.8
Prior year funds and other financial adjustments	−1.7	−2.9	−1.5

Source: *The Budget of the United States Government, Fiscal Year 1971*, p. 84.

place, but the specific contingencies and force level determinations connected with this policy have not yet been forthcoming, at least in public sources.

Strategic Nuclear Forces

Assured destruction apparently remains the object toward which the strategic forces are principally directed. As the budget puts it, "Our strategic forces are designed to provide a highly reliable and credible ability to inflict unacceptable damage upon those who might attempt a nuclear attack upon the United States or its allies."[1] The President asked, however, in his February message whether, in a retaliatory strike, he should "be left with the single option of ordering the mass destruction of enemy civilians, in the face of the certainty that it would be followed by the mass slaughter of Americans. Should the concept of assured destruction be narrowly defined and should it be the only measure of our ability to deter the variety of threats we may face?"[2]

The proposal to continue deployment of Safeguard makes clear the desire for at least some damage-limiting capability, presumably against mainland China. The AWACS-F-106X air defense system is also under development as a replacement for the present obsolescent SAGE–BUIC system, supposedly at only slightly higher procurement and operating cost over the next decade. Though the Safeguard sites programmed for Malmstrom, Montana; Grand Forks, North Dakota; Warren, Wyoming; and Whiteman, Missouri (all Air Force bases) will afford a measure of protection to land-based ICBMs and some bombers, what principally seems to be involved is an effort to force the Soviet Union, which is likely to be uncertain of the effectiveness of Safeguard, to choose between a major expansion of its SS-9 program and abandoning any hope of acquiring the ability to destroy our land-based ICBMs. With respect to the ABM's role as a protector of the civilian population, Safeguard will be able at best—and at very considerable cost—to deal with very light attacks.

Turning to strategic offensive forces, the President proposes to continue perfecting MIRV technology and to deploy MIRVs on the new missiles soon to be introduced into the forces, Minuteman III and Poseidon. He plans a modest acceleration of the ULMS research and development program to provide a sea-based platform for large, long-range missiles should the SS-9 buildup continue and pose a serious threat to land-based missiles that Safeguard cannot handle. The budget also proposes to proceed with short-range attack missiles (SRAMs) that would give the bomber force the capability to attack targets from outside sophisticated short-range defenses. The AMSA is continued at only a relatively low level of effort as a replacement for the B-52. In short, survivability and penetration receive the bulk of attention in the offensive programs.

Each of these investments in strategic nuclear systems, offensive and defensive, raises five separate but related issues. First is the issue of the goals toward which the entire strategic establishment is directed, the criteria by which it is judged, and the specific contribution of each system. Second, there is the technical question, particularly relevant in the case of Safeguard, whether the system will work at all and, if so, at what level of effectiveness and cost. Third, it must be asked whether each system represents the best buy when compared with other possibilities. Fourth, the government must decide which systems represent blue chips at SALT and which tactic—acceleration or restraint—is most likely to produce the desired Soviet response. Finally, and closely related to SALT strategy, this country must try to foresee the effect of each decision on the attitudes of present and potential holders of nuclear weapons, particularly but not exclusively the Soviet Union and mainland China.

Of course the chemistry of the U.S.-Soviet relation is the most sensitive and important of these issues, and because of it, we need constant reminding that U.S. options will change with time. The decision to proceed with MIRVs, for example, even though—or perhaps because—SALT resumes in April, raises a serious question. Will the United States be able to join with the USSR in a verifiable ban on MIRVs, should it so desire, given the difficulty of unilaterally verifying the absence of these weapons when it is known they have been tested and can be deployed? A failure to ban MIRVs, even at this late date, may be a genuine tragedy if agreement might otherwise have been possible. Yet to propose that we forego further MIRV testing requires two judgments: that in the short run a cessation of testing would not lead to an unacceptable risk for the U.S. strategic position, and that in the longer run there is a reasonable chance that such an action on our part would induce a similar Soviet response.

These judgments are important to the basic reconsideration of strategic policy that the times clearly demand. If the United States adopts a minimal view of what it takes to deter the Soviet Union and possibly other nuclear nations from attacks on this country and its allies, it follows that with the very large forces already at our disposal we can afford to defer further major programs—such as MIRVs, the ABM, and AMSA—in order to test the will to arms limitations and at the same time to save money for other pressing needs. If, on the other hand, we decide that assured destruction alone is not a credible deterrent, then we must demonstrate the capacity, in the event of an enemy attack, to carry out something other than a suicidal attack on his cities—for example, a strike against his missile sites or military bases—particularly if we want our allies to refrain from nuclear investments. And this, in turn, may require some margin of striking power above a substantial retaliatory capability. These issues and the five preceding ones related above are in sore need of systematic consideration. There is no evidence in the 1971 budget that they have yet been decided. The strategic programs in this budget represent a modest restatement and continuation of previous policies.

General Purpose Forces

Much the same can be said of the budget for general purpose forces. To the extent that it reveals a rationale, the logic remains essentially the same as it was in 1969 and 1970—the need for versatility and the ability to follow a wide range of strategies other than general nuclear war. If this is the case, it would mean baseline forces comprising on the order of sixteen and one-third Army divisions and three Marine divisions, essentially the same National Guard and reserve forces as before, twenty-three wings of Air Force fighter-bombers, fifteen attack carriers with their air wings, 239 ASW and AAW escorts, more than sixty nuclear attack submarines (SSNs), including at least six of the new high-speed variety, four ASW carriers to be outfitted with the new S-3A aircraft, along with at least 300 land-based patrol aircraft, and a large force of amphibious assault ships, minesweepers, and fire support ships. The strategic airlift will presumably stop at fourteen squadrons of C-141s and four squadrons of C-5As; the sealift will probably remain out of balance with the airlift unless the Congress approves Secretary Laird's recent proposal to construct the equivalent of fast deployment logistics ships (FDLs) under charter arrangements.

Although the baseline general purpose forces have undergone a modest reduction as a result of base closures, the mothballing of older ships, and the retirement of aging aircraft, they bear a striking resem-

blance to the pre-Vietnam baseline force. Yet Secretary Laird has
hinted in his 1970 posture statement, and newspaper reports have
asserted, that a major change in the baseline force is in the offing.
Secretary Laird states flatly that we never have had the capability to
cope simultaneously with two major contingencies and one minor
contingency, and that "under our new strategy we will maintain in
peacetime General Purpose Forces that are adequate for simultaneously meeting a major communist attack in either Europe or in
Asia, assisting allies to cope with non-Chinese threats in Asia, and
in addition, meeting a contingency elsewhere."[3]

Less formal descriptions of the new strategy suggest that we plan to
dispense with many of the baseline forces now supposedly associated
with the Asian contingency and perhaps even revert to a greater dependence—at least for "jawboning" purposes—on the tactical use of
nuclear weapons. Such a change could mean a substantial reduction in
the cost of the baseline general purpose forces. It would also mean a
somewhat greater risk—particularly if land forces and strategic mobility were the first to be cut—since there is great uncertainty as to
just how many forces are needed for any major contingency. Consequently an issue for the future, if not for 1971, is the extent to which
changes in general purpose forces should be rigidly related to changes
in the number of contingencies for which we prepare, and how many
of these forces we really want to dispense with as a result of the Guam
doctrine.

In his message on United States foreign policy for the 1970s, the
President indicated that the new strategy is an "effort to harmonize
doctrine and capability." To the extent that this foreshadows a reduction in baseline general purpose forces, it could have one of several
results. First, the United States might exercise much greater restraint
in committing and deploying its military power. Second, it might simply avoid becoming committed simultaneously on two fronts, the
prospects of which, in the President's view, "are low both because of
the risks of nuclear war and the improbability of Sino-Soviet coopera-
tion." Third, we might place greater reliance on our theater nuclear
forces. Indeed, there is at least the hint of such an intention in the
President's statement that "the nuclear capability of our strategic and
theater nuclear forces serves as a deterrent to full-scale Soviet attack
on NATO Europe or Chinese attack on our Asian allies," and in his
suggestion that, in the unlikely event of combined Sino-Soviet aggres-

sion, "we do not believe that such a coordinated attack should be met primarily by U.S. conventional forces."[4]

In these circumstances, we need to ask how serious we really are about substituting tactical nuclear weapons for conventional forces and warfare. During the past fifteen years the case for such a substitution has failed to withstand systematic examination. If there are serious new arguments for believing that the theater nuclear forces provide the United States with some advantage heretofore unrealized, it is important to examine them.

Whatever may be decided with respect to the future size of the general purpose forces, there remain a great many issues concerning their specific composition. One of the most urgent has to do with tactical air capability. If the Air Force, Navy, and Marine Corps wings are all counted as part of that capability, it costs about $14 billion a year and provides more than forty-one fighter-attack wings. At least 30 percent of this capability is intended for deep interdiction of enemy lines of communication, despite the fact that experience in Korea and Vietnam has raised an increasing challenge to the utility of interdiction sorties. There is also a question whether more than twelve attack carriers are needed, requiring that we keep buying new attack carrier task forces at an investment cost of more than $1.8 billion apiece, despite the availability of land bases in the main theaters where the United States is heavily committed. There is the related question whether the proposed F-14 and F-15 Navy and Air Force fighters are the best possible successors to the F-4, and the rate at which the F-4s should be replaced.

A great many other issues concerning the general purpose forces are already subjects of intense debate among defense analysts. They have to do with the future utility of large amphibious forces, the need for ASW carriers and diesel-powered submarines, the advantages of large and very expensive destroyers rather than destroyer escorts, the extent to which the new main battle tank makes sense as a replacement for the M-60, and such detailed matters as the wisdom of continuing to add electronic equipment with low reliability to aircraft and to substitute missiles for guns on armored vehicles.

As equipment and its maintenance grow increasingly expensive, still other questions arise. At any given budget level, are we willing to accept supposedly advanced technology as a substitute for numbers? For example, do we really believe that one F-14 is the equivalent of two or three F-4s? Alternatively, with rapidly rising costs and presumed increases in effectiveness, is it necessary to replace existing aircraft, ships, helicopters, and tanks on a one-for-one basis? And in what may be an era of declining defense budgets, are we willing to sacrifice combat readiness in the short run so as to continue paying for new equipment with high technology and long lead-times? Should we forego the costs of sonobuoys and torpedoes, ordnance and rockets, spare parts and maintenance manpower, at a risk to sustained combat effectiveness, until such time as defense budgets become more generous? Does it make sense to keep large land forces in the United States if we are not also willing to maintain enough airlift and sealift to move them to areas of commitment in a timely fashion?

When the bills for such imbalances come due, they tend to be very high indeed. Cutting the defense budget therefore involves not only a question of how much, but also where. Whether or not a further decline in defense spending is desirable, if we still care about the military effectiveness of the U.S. defense establishment we must learn to be as concerned about the distribution of defense dollars as we are about the absolute size of the expenditures. The 1971 budget provides little new guidance on either.

Vietnam Disengagement

Table 2-7 shows the reductions in defense personnel in 1970 and 1971, most of which are attributable to disengagement from Vietnam.

It seems plausible to infer from the budget that about $6 billion in Vietnam war costs will be saved in 1971 compared with the previous year. The main budgetary issue with respect to Vietnam is, of course, the rate of troop withdrawals. If the armed force reductions called for

Table 2-7. Personnel Strength, Department of Defense, Fiscal Years 1969–71[a]

Fiscal year	Military personnel	Reduc-tion	Civilian personnel	Reduc-tion
1969 (actual)	3,459,423	...	1,225,877	...
1970 (estimate)	3,160,700	298,723	1,165,900	59,977
1971 (estimate)	2,908,100	252,600	1,110,000	55,800
Total reduction (estimate)	...	551,323	...	115,777

Source: *Special Analyses, Budget of the United States, Fiscal Year 1971*, pp. 100, 102.
a. All figures are as of the end of the fiscal year to which they relate.

in the budget primarily reflect withdrawals from Vietnam, this would seem to imply the removal of about 180,000 men from the theater and a further reduction of perhaps 60,000 or more along the line of communication and within the United States. This would leave about 200,000 men in Vietnam by the end of 1971. Judging from other administration statements, however, the budget numbers should not be taken to reflect an inviolable schedule of withdrawal.

Long-Term Implications

To say that major issues of long-term strategic and general purpose force policy have not been decided is not to suggest that the defense budget for fiscal 1971 ignores them. As the disengagement from Vietnam continues, major units are being disbanded and the defense establishment is shrinking. As indicated in the following section, many programs that had previously come under fire have been cancelled or severely curtailed. Nevertheless, it remains true that the defense budget as yet commits the administration to no clear course for the longer term.

Critics will argue that the budget contains the seed money for a rapid growth in expenditures on future weapon systems, and they may be right. About 130 new systems, estimated to involve a total procurement cost of at least $140 billion, are under development or in procurement, and new systems, once started, have proved notoriously difficult to cancel. As the cost of hardware increases by a factor of two or more, the United States could end up with higher budgets, less manpower, and lower fighting effectiveness.

This is not, however, a necessary result. Although programs such as the F-14, the F-15, AMSA, AWACS, and Safeguard would increase future budgets if they were added on top of everything else and rapidly procured, this outcome is by no means preordained. As new systems are brought into the active inventory, older systems with high operating costs can be retired, although there is usually a lag between new procurement and the phasing out of the older systems. Moreover, the rate of deployment of the new systems will determine whether there are sharp increases in the appropriations for military personnel, operations and maintenance, and procurement. Programs can be bunched up or stretched out, depending on the actions of potential adversaries, the fiscal situation, and the other uses to which the President and the Congress may wish to put federal resources. Except in special circumstances, as when there was concern about a "missile gap," the cycle of modernization and replacement can be regulated without undue domestic or foreign repercussions. Theories to the contrary notwithstanding, the defense budget is not uncontrollable in the same sense as social security.

Thus, fiscal 1971 can be the harbinger of further declines in defense spending or it can serve as the basis for very rapid increases in the future. Since new funding authority is falling behind expected outlays, there is some indication that the administration expects defense spending in the next year or two to fall still further. And if the intent is to disengage from Vietnam during 1971 and 1972 and revert substantially to the pre-Vietnam baseline force, it is easy to imagine a defense outlay (in 1975 prices) approaching $75 billion or less by 1975—not much higher than the present budget and about $10 billion lower in today's prices. A rather literal interpretation of the Guam doctrine and a very restrained strategic posture could result in considerably lower expenditures—about $49 billion in present prices and about $58 billion in prices likely to prevail in 1975.

This, however, is all speculation. Defense budgets are the product not only of specific calculation, but also of the vagaries of international and domestic politics. We probably shall not know what kind of five-year program the administration intends to adopt until at least 1972. Even then, as in the past, defense budgets will be highly sensitive to year-to-year considerations. Nevertheless, barring extraordinary events and confrontations, a reasonable guess would be that the trend of defense spending will be down during the next few years.

Selected Special Issues

The alternatives posed in the foregoing discussion have been presented in the broadest of terms in order briefly to summarize possible general outlines of defense spending as part of a larger framework of national priorities. There are, however, a great many difficult and controversial issues within each estimate. Some, such as the question of the efficacy of the ABM, receive a great deal of public attention. Others tend to be neglected. The following sections offer short treatments of four specific issues that perhaps receive too little attention in the public debate: the relationship of general purpose forces to various contingencies, the general magnitude of savings that could be realized by applying cost-benefit criteria, the incremental cost of the Vietnam war, and the question of a "deferred deficit" of defense needs that must be met when the war is over.

Allocation of the Baseline General Purpose Forces by Contingency

What would be the implications for the general purpose forces if the United States abandoned the strategic concept of preparing for two major wars and one minor conflict? What would happen if we designed instead for one major and one minor war? The answer turns to an important degree on whether the general purpose forces (whose size and composition as of fiscal 1965 are shown in Table 2-8) ever had the capability simultaneously to fight two major wars and one minor engagement. But it also depends on how the forces relate to specific contingencies.

European Contingencies

During the 1960s, the assumption with respect to Europe was that NATO could deter an attack by the Warsaw Pact and that it could sustain an adequate forward defense, particularly in Germany, provided that certain conditions were met. First, NATO would have to maintain approximate equality with the Pact in deployed land and tactical air forces within the theater—defined as Western and Eastern Europe but not, for the most part, the Soviet Union itself. Second, NATO should be able to match the Pact in its ability to mobilize and deploy additional active and reserve forces. Third, NATO should be able to sustain its forces with supplies, equipment, and manpower replacements for at least as long as the Warsaw Pact, and preferably for an indefinite period. In sum, the assumption has been that NATO should have the capability to fight a major non-nuclear war with the Warsaw Pact countries.

As of 1968, according to the Defense Department, the deployed NATO and Pact forces in Western and Eastern Europe were about equal in manpower except in the area of Norway. NATO, including the French, had about 900,000 troops deployed in all regions of Continental Europe, compared to 960,000 troops for the Pact. NATO had about 2,100 aircraft deployed, as against 2,900 deployed for the

Table 2-8. Composition of the Major Active Armed Forces Units: The General Purpose Forces as of June 30, 1965

Item	Actual number
Total military personnel	2,655,389
General purpose forces	
Army divisions (combat ready)	16
Army armored cavalry regiments	4
Army special forces groups	7
Marine Corps divisions	3
Marine Corps air wings	3
Warships	
Attack carriers	15
Antisubmarine warfare carriers	9
Nuclear attack submarines	21
Other warships	331
Amphibious assault ships (in commission)	135
Carrier air groups (attack and antisubmarine warfare)	28
Air Force tactical squadrons	117
Airlift and sealift forces	
Airlift squadrons	
C-130, C-133, C-135, C-141	38
C-118, C-119, C-123, C-124	19
Troopships, cargo ships, and tankers	106
Active aircraft inventory, all programs:	
Army	6,957
Navy	8,056
Air Force	14,875
Commissioned ships in fleet, all programs	880

Source: *The Budget of the United States Government for the Fiscal Year Ending June 30, 1967*, p. 76.

Warsaw Pact, in the crucial Center Region. Thus, although a precise balance did not exist in land and tactical air forces, it has been argued that a U.S. deployment of four and one-third divisions, seven wings of tactical aircraft, and two attack carriers in the Mediterranean is a sufficient contribution to the forward, deployed defense of Western Europe. The theory has been that to the extent that more very expensive, deployed, immediately usable (M-day) forces might be needed, the other NATO allies should provide them.

As far as reinforcing capabilities were concerned, the conclusion was:

If either side chose, the ready land forces could be greatly reinforced before any fighting began (as in the 1961 Berlin Crisis). Assuming a simultaneous mobilization, within 30 days the Pact could probably gain a manpower advantage on the Central Front [facing Germany] and a somewhat greater advantage in overall ground combat capability. This gap would then begin to narrow with the arrival of more U.S. forces. NATO tactical aircraft reinforcements would about equal the Pact's in the early stages of mobilization, after which we could add considerably more aircraft than the Pact.[5]

It is impossible to state precisely the necessary U.S. contribution to such a mobilization and deployment. But available data suggest rather strongly that the European members of NATO, and the East European members of the Pact, would not have more than a few additional divisions and air wings to contribute to the forces already deployed in the first ninety days of this mobilization. Thus, the United States and the USSR would have to provide the bulk of the reinforcements.

Taking into account current Soviet deployments in Eastern Europe and the Far East, and what the USSR might deploy into Eastern Europe over a period of ninety days or so, about eleven additional U.S. division forces and perhaps another nine air wings would be required to match them. Not all of these reinforcing divisions would have to be in the active inventory; perhaps as many as seven could be in the reserve, provided that they were kept in sufficiently high readiness to permit callup and deployment within six to eight weeks.

Thus it was determined that a total of about fifteen active and reserve division forces and twenty-one tactical air wings (counting one Marine wing, the two attack carriers in the Mediterranean, and two others in the Atlantic) would represent the cutting edge of the U.S. contribution to NATO. But this by no means constituted the full requirement that would be generated by a major contingency in Europe. Additional capabilities were considered essential, including:

1. Enough amphibious assault ships to lift and land the assault echelons of one Marine expeditionary force (a division/wing team) in the Atlantic, with half of this force lifted by fast (20-knot) modern ships.

2. Sufficient prepositioned equipment, airlift, and sealift to permit timely reinforcement of our forces in Europe at the same time that we engaged in a rapid deployment to Southeast Asia. This meant a total programmed force—as calculated in 1968—of six squadrons of C-5A aircraft, fourteen squadrons of C-141s, and thirty fast deployment logistic ships; prepositioned equipment for several divisions in Europe

and a brigade in the Pacific; a Civil Reserve air fleet; and 460 commercial cargo ships. While all of this lift could be used and might actually be needed in one major theater, it seems fair to assume that, in the baseline force, about half of it could be attributed to the NATO contingency.

3. War reserve stocks of combat consumables, weapons, and equipment sufficient to permit the forces to fight at high rates of consumption for about three months. This meant preparing to fight a non-nuclear war of about three months' duration, provided that the allies were prepared (which experience has suggested they are not) to maintain adequate war reserves of their own.

4. Protection of the line of communications between the United States and Europe and protection of the fleet by means of attack submarines, land-based patrol aircraft, ASW carriers, ASW escort vessels, and AAW escorts that would be emplaced between enemy submarines and their targets. By such a deployment, according to official sources, "we would be able to destroy a very large proportion of the Soviet submarine force in a matter of a few months, while losing only a relatively small part of the Free World merchant fleet."[6] The strategy also called for close-in protection of the fleet and convoys. The worldwide forces required for this strategy were programmed to comprise about 105 attack submarines, of which sixty were to be "first-class" nuclear submarines (SSNs), around thirty squadrons of land-based patrol aircraft, eight ASW carriers (now reduced to four), and 239 ASW and AAW escorts. Despite these large numbers, however, it was pointed out that "to meet the merchant ship convoy requirement, we plan to rely on the large number of escort ships in our reserve fleet and in the naval forces of our allies . . . [who] have about 400 destroyer-type ships in their active fleets."[7] Of this very large, worldwide U.S. force, about half is based in the Atlantic and is mainly a charge against the European contingency.

5. Nuclear forces in the theater to deter the use of nuclear weapons by the Warsaw Pact and for possible use in the event that the Soviet Union should begin a tactical nuclear engagement, or that a conventional attack should begin to overwhelm the non-nuclear defenses of NATO. In Europe alone, more than 7,000 nuclear weapons are deployed for possible use by the NATO allies as well as by U.S. forces, and it has been estimated that there are about 2,500 nuclear

delivery systems available, ranging from tactical aircraft and Pershing missiles to short-range rockets and artillery. The yield of these tactical weapons varies from a fraction of a kiloton to 100 kilotons or more. The basis on which this formidable armory has been justified is not a matter of public record, but it seems plausible to assume that the inventory reflects at least some calculation about the number and types of targets that would require attack.

Asian Contingencies

While the defense of Europe was clearly the contingency that generated the largest demand for U.S. general purpose forces, and though a theater like the Middle East might also make a claim on these resources, it was Asia—and particularly our commitments in Korea and Southeast Asia—that generated the next greatest potential demand for U.S. forces. These commitments, combined with the hostility expected of China, made it plausible to use the possibility of conflict in Asia as the second major contingency for which to plan the force structure. If the United States could deal simultaneously with the opening phases of wars in Europe and Asia, the resulting capabilities would constitute a conservatively designed general purpose force, however and wherever we might decide to use it.

The principal threats in Asia were considered to be conventional attacks by the North Koreans and North Vietnamese, supported by the Chinese. In early 1968 and probably in 1970 as well, the active land forces of those three countries contained the following manpower:[8]

Country	Number of men in active land forces
China	2,351,000
North Korea	345,000
North Vietnam	442,000
Total	3,138,000

In the aggregate, the tactical air forces of these countries were also large. But, as was pointed out, "the Asian Communists have limited offensive air ability. The MIG-15s, 17s, and 19s, comprising 85 percent of the Chinese Air Force, cannot attack targets much beyond the borders of China because of their limited range and the location of Chinese airfields."[9]

Although the types of forces required for an Asian contingency were the same as in Europe, the effort to achieve equality in land forces seemed neither feasible nor necessary. Substantial Chinese forces remained tied down in Manchuria and opposite Taiwan. Because of severe logistical constraints, it seemed likely that they would "have only a limited ability to attack beyond their borders,"[10] and the idea that the Chinese could simultaneously launch attacks in Korea and Southeast Asia was heavily discounted. Moreover, it was remembered that in Korea "the last major Chinese offensive (825,000 men) was stopped by a force of some 535,000."[11] The U.S. contingent at that time consisted of about seven divisions and 500 fighter/attack aircraft. Since then, of course, forces of the Republic of Korea have expanded very substantially and improved greatly in quality. Nevertheless, two U.S. divisions have remained in Korea as part of the Asian contingency force.

The forces needed for Southeast Asia proved even more difficult to compute than those required for Europe. Not only was it hard to define likely contingencies, but there was also a problem in determining the number and type of enemy forces that could be supported over difficult lines of communication that might to some degree be interdicted. However, it was considered plausible—at least by some—that because of the enormous U.S. advantages in firepower, mobility, and logistical support, no more than eight U.S. divisions (counting the two in Korea), about three attack carrier wings, seven Air Force fighter/attack wings, and two Marine wings would suffice, in conjunction with allied forces, to block the main avenues of attack into Vietnam, Laos, and Thailand. As it turned out, the war in Vietnam came to absorb more than ten divisions and 1,150 fighter/attack aircraft based in South Vietnam and Thailand and aboard carriers offshore. However, this was said to demonstrate the utility rather than the defects of planning because "we used the forces earmarked for a major Asian contingency to meet the immediate needs in the summer of 1965 and then activated temporary forces to meet the longer range needs."[12] In other words, while two Army divisions remained in Korea, four Army divisions and two Marine divisions moved into Vietnam to provide the screen behind which the mobilization and deployment of new forces could occur.

As in the case of Europe, an Asian contingency generated the demand for enough amphibious assault ships to lift and land the assault echelons of one Marine expeditionary force, although the rationale for this type and size of force was primarily historical. Several thousand nuclear weapons were also deployed in the Pacific, presumably for the same reasons and on the same calculations that had inspired their prepositioning in Europe. ASW and AAW forces were similarly said to be needed to protect the long line of communications to Asia, as well as the fleet, although it was not clear who would threaten them. And war reserve stocks had to be maintained at levels sufficient to replenish supplies and equipment until such time as the production base could provide them.

The planners considered airlift and sealift particularly important for an Asian contingency:

> The ability to respond promptly to clear threats to our national interests and the security of our allies, possibly in more than one place at the same time, can serve both to deter and to prevent such threats from expanding into larger conflicts. There are essentially two main approaches, bracketing a broad range of alternatives, by which this capability can be provided. The first is to maintain very large conventional forces stationed around the globe near all potential trouble spots. The second is to maintain a smaller central reserve of highly ready forces supported by the lift capability required to deploy them promptly to wherever they might be needed.[18]

By contrast with the Korean experience, when it took fifty-six days to deploy the first U.S.-based division, it was apparently hoped that with modern airlift and sea-lift in the numbers and types programmed, it might become possible to deploy as many as six divisions to Southeast Asia in thirty days.

There is an element of arbitrariness and uncertainty in attempting to break down general purpose forces by regions, but as interest in the general purpose forces has become more widespread, questions have arisen about both the burden assumed by the United States overseas and the contingencies for which we prepare. Consequently, Table 2-9 summarizes the previous discussion and shows the forces that are either deployed to or earmarked for a particular theater. Table 2-10 provides a rough idea of the average annual cost of these forces and contingencies.

This review makes clear the basis for debate about the readiness of general purpose forces to meet likely contingencies. The pre-Vietnam baseline force is definitely designed to meet the two-and-a-half war pattern, but in important part through mobility of U.S.-based reserves rather than foreign-deployed standing forces. Moreover, the

Table 2-9. Distribution of Baseline General Purpose Forces by Geographic Contingency as of 1970

Type of force	Europe	Asia	Other areas	Strategic Reserve
Active divisions (Army and Marine Corps)	8	8	1	2⅓
National Guard and Reserve divisions	7	...	...	2
Navy tactical air wings[a]	4	6	1	4
Marine air wings	1	2	1	...
Air Force tactical air wings	16	7	...	...
ASW and AAW forces	half	half	...	...
Amphibious and other forces	one-third	two-thirds	...	...
Airlift and sealift forces	half	half	...	...
Research and development	...	...	...	all

Sources: *Statement of Secretary of Defense Robert S. McNamara before the Senate Armed Services Committee on the Fiscal Year 1969-73 Defense Program and 1969 Defense Budget,* U.S. Department of Defense (Jan. 22, 1968), pp. 77-86; *Statement of Secretary of Defense Clark M. Clifford: The Fiscal Year 1970-74 Defense Program and 1970 Defense Budget,* U.S. Department of Defense (Jan. 15, 1969), pp. 30, 79; The Institute for Strategic Studies, *The Military Balance, 1969-1970,* pp. 3-5, 7-10, 11, 14-18, 38-40; Alain C. Enthoven, "Arms and Men: The Military Balance in Europe," *Interplay,* Vol. 2, No. 10 (May 1969), pp. 11-14; Alain C. Enthoven and K. Wayne Smith, "What Forces for NATO? And from Whom?" *Foreign Affairs,* Vol. 48, No. 1 (October 1969), pp. 80-96; *Status of Naval Ships,* Hearings before the Special Subcommittee on Sea Power of the House Committee on Armed Services (1969), pp. 288, 336-42.
a. All carriers on station (two in the Atlantic, three in the Pacific) and their immediate back-up carriers are allocated to Europe and Asia.

Table 2-10. Allocation of Costs of Baseline General Purpose Forces by Geographic Contingency, Fiscal Year 1971[a]

Billions of 1971 dollars

Type of force	Europe	Asia	Other areas	Strategic Reserve	Total cost
Active divisions (Army and Marine Corps)[b]	6.4	6.4	0.8	1.9	15.5
National Guard and Reserve divisions	2.0	...	...	0.5	2.5
Navy tactical air wings	1.9	2.8	0.5	1.9	7.1
Air Force tactical air wings	4.6	2.3	...	...	6.9
ASW and AAW forces[c]	2.5	2.5	...	...	5.0
Amphibious and other forces	0.7	1.3	...	...	2.0
Airlift and sealift forces	1.0	1.0	...	...	2.0
Research and development	...	...	...	3.0	3.0
Total	19.1	16.3	1.3	7.3	44.0

Sources: *Statement of Secretary of Defense Robert S. McNamara before the House Armed Services Committee on the Fiscal Year 1965-69 Defense Program and 1965 Defense Budget,* U.S. Department of Defense (Jan. 27, 1964), pp. 166-69; *Statement of Secretary of Defense Clark M. Clifford: The Fiscal Year 1970-74 Defense Program and 1970 Defense Budget,* U.S. Department of Defense (Jan. 15, 1969), p. 157; testimony of John S. Foster, Jr., in *Status of U.S. Strategic Power,* Hearings before the Preparedness Investigating Subcommittee of the Senate Committee on Armed Services, 90 Cong. 2 sess. (1968), Part 1, p. 109; testimony of Thomas H. Moorer, in *Authorization for Military Procurement, Research and Development, Fiscal Year 1970, and Reserve Strength,* Hearings before the Senate Committee on Armed Services, 91 Cong. 1 sess. (1969), Part 1, pp. 667, 680; *St. Louis Post Dispatch,* Jan. 6, 1963; J. G. Fish and A. L. Doyle, *Cost of War Index,* Douglas Missile and Space Systems Division, McDonnell Douglas Corporation, Santa Monica, California (September 1968), DAC-58166, pp. 39-206.
a. Excluding the incremental costs of the war in Vietnam.
b. Including Marine air wings.
c. Excluding escorts for the attack carriers.

present strategy assumes higher levels of allied preparedness than have ever actually been approached, as well as capabilities for mainland China that some believe are subject to challenge. Both the President and Secretary Laird have on several recent occasions suggested that the planning base has shifted or will be shifted to the one-and-a-half war alternative, but the 1971 budget does not reflect this in any decisive manner.

Cost and Effectiveness: Microstrategic Issues

This review has been concerned mostly with what might be termed "macrostrategic" analysis in which types of forces are largely taken as given and are matched against alternative objectives, using such large aggregates as divisions and wings. However, most of the professional analysis that has become familiar during the past decade has focused on so-called "microstrategic" issues of optimal size, composition, and cost of forces within the constraint of objectives taken as given. These issues are very significant from both substantive and budgetary points of view, for concepts of opportunity cost and marginal utility are just as important in defense programs as elsewhere in the budget.

Many microstrategic issues already have extensive histories. The question of larger strategic nuclear forces has led to the calculation that beyond the optimal delivery of 400 one-megaton weapons— which would produce 74 million deaths (30 percent of the population) and destroy 76 percent of industrial capacity in the Soviet Union— it would take a doubling of megatons to raise the level of damage by 9 percent. On another front, the question of a new strategic bomber (AMSA) has yielded the view, apparently shared by the present secretary of defense and his predecessors, that replacement of the B-52 with something beyond the new FB-111 is not as urgent as development of new weapons and penetration devices. Similar questions have arisen with respect to the effectiveness of ASW carriers; the optimal number of Air Force fighter/attack wings in the baseline force in the light of concern about the utility of interdiction bombing; the balance between Navy and Air Force fighter/attack wings; and ways of increasing the use of the Army helicopter inventory. In addition, of course, major issues have arisen with respect to the effectiveness of strategic defenses (particularly the Safeguard ABM system), the merits of a hardpoint defense of land-based ICBMs as against increments of submarine-based missiles, and the extent to which other and cheaper penetration aids can do the job of MIRVs.

It is noteworthy that a number of measures to increase efficiency and eliminate waste have recently been taken, including a reduction in the continental air defense system, sizable manpower cuts, elimination of the Mark II electronics system for the F-111D, cancellation of the Cheyenne helicopter, mothballing of more than 100 ships—including four ASW carriers and several amphibious assault vessels—and cancellation of the manned orbital laboratory (MOL). Nonetheless, many analysts would include on a current list of microstrategic issues a number of other items, such as Safeguard, FDLs (fast deployment logistic ships), new assault ships (LHAs), and the status of at least three of the older attack carriers. Some might add to it Minuteman III, the AWACS-F-106X combination, the main battle tank (MBT-70), major helicopter procurement, the new nuclear attack carriers CVAN-69 and CVAN-70, the F-14 Navy fighter, the carrier-based S-3A ASW patrol aircraft, the "high-speed" submarines, the destroyer class DD-963, and the F-15 Air Force fighter—at least as it is now designed.

It is difficult to estimate how much the cancellation or deferral of these programs would save over the next five years. Cancellation might simply mean the substitution of other less expensive programs—as in the cases of the F-14 and F-15—or the continuation of existing programs at increasingly high cost in operation and maintenance. The cost of continuing new programs is equally difficult to estimate, since the pace of development and procurement is another matter of choice. The 1971 budget anticipates new funds amounting to about $19.5 billion for operation and maintenance, $17.4 billion for procurement, and $7.3 billion for research, development, testing, and evaluation. These amounts are about the same as the pre-Vietnam baseline allowances for comparable categories inflated to current prices. Thus they still allow for the introduction of a number of expensive new weapon systems, particularly if the process is gradual and does not replace the older systems on a one-for-one basis.

Nonetheless, it seems plausible to assume that a fairly rigorous pruning of the more questionable new programs could result in net savings of about $3 billion by 1975, over and above those achieved from major force reductions. It should be added that, while such pruning could take place at many different budgeting levels, cuts tend to be easier and more obvious when defense outlays are high than when they become more austere.

The Incremental Cost of the Vietnam War

The actual growth and gradual decline of U.S. military manpower in Vietnam is readily ascertainable, as shown in Tables 2-11 and 2-15. At the end of 1961 the total U.S. military presence amounted to 3,200 men. By the end of 1963, the number had risen to 16,300. Thereafter the total climbed rapidly to a peak of about 538,200 in June 1969. Since then, the President has announced troop withdrawals that will amount to 115,500 men by April 15, 1970. It would be reasonable to expect that at least another 30,000 men have been taken out of the line of communications and support activities in the United States.

Other data about the U.S. war effort are also available. About 800,000 military personnel and 250,000 civilians were added to the defense establishment as a direct result of the war. At the peak of our involvement we deployed to Vietnam on the order of ten and two-thirds Army and Marine Corps division forces, 1,150 aircraft on land and on offshore attack carriers, as well as Special Forces, Coast Guard, and other naval units. The peak of the fighting consumed over 2.5 million tons a year of ground ammunition, air ordnance, and naval gun ammunition. Between January 1, 1961 and the end of December 1969, the United States lost a total of 6,290 aircraft and helicopters in the area from all causes. At their peak, of fixed-wing aircraft losses in Southeast Asia exceeded 500 planes a year.

Table 2-11. U.S. Military Personnel in the Vietnam Conflict, Various Years, 1961–69[a]

Forces	1961–62	1964	1965	1966	1967	1968	1969
Army	10,000	14,700	116,800	239,400	319,500	359,800	361,500
Navy[b]	600	1,100	8,400	23,300	31,700	36,100	35,500
Marine Corps	500	900	38,200	69,200	78,000	81,400	79,900
Air Force	3,400	6,600	20,600	52,900	55,900	58,400	60,800
Coast Guard	...	...	300	500	500	400	500
Total	14,500	23,300	185,300	385,300	485,600	536,100	538,200

Source: U.S. Bureau of the Census, *Statistical Abstract of the United States: 1969*, p. 256.
a. All figures are as of the end of the calendar year except those for 1969, which are as of March 30.
b. Excludes personnel on ships offshore.

But how do all these figures translate into costs directly attributable to the war? On February 14, 1968, Secretary McNamara testified that "the incremental cost of Vietnam is on the order of $17 to $20 billion."[14] He reached this estimate on the basis of two assumptions: that the baseline force would cost about $60 billion in 1969 prices; that funds were not being diverted from the baseline force to pay for the war; and, therefore, that the difference between baseline costs and the total defense budget would represent the incremental cost of the war.

The present defense comptroller has arrived at quite a different set of figures. He distributes the defense budget between the costs of operations in Southeast Asia and those of the baseline force as shown in Table 2-12. The comptroller's figures clearly suggest not only that funds have been diverted from the baseline force to pay for the war, but also that there is a very large backlog of deferred requirements that must be made up if the baseline force is to return to its level of effectiveness prior to the major expansion of the war. In the comptroller's words: "This sharp drop in . . . non-Southeast Asia costs was in large part deliberate, to ease the impact of the war upon the economy. The effect, however, has been to create a series of backlogs and deferrals—a slowdown in training and operating tempos for our forces elsewhere, deferral of modernization and maintenance, etc. There has been no major decline in our missions and defense requirements in other parts of the world, and these backlogs present a serious problem."[15]

The comptroller seems to be suggesting, in other words, that even if we revert to the pre-Vietnam baseline force when the war ends, the

Table 2-12. The Defense Comptroller's Estimates of Expenditures on Southeast Asia Forces and the Baseline Force, Fiscal Years 1965–70

Billions of current dollars

Category	1965	1966	1967	1968	1969	1970
Southeast Asia forces	0.1	5.8	20.1	26.5	28.8	24.9
Baseline force	47.0	49.4	48.2	51.5	49.6	53.0
Total outlay	47.1	55.2	68.3	78.0	78.4	77.9

Source: Testimony of Robert C. Moot in *The Military Budget and National Economic Priorities*, Hearings before the Subcommittee on Economy in Government of the Joint Economic Committee, 91 Cong. 1 sess. (1969), Part 1, p. 320.

baseline budget must be increased by $3 billion or $4 billion a year. Calculations of incremental cost are always difficult, and that of the Vietnam war is particularly elusive because there were strong incentives to charge baseline expenditures against the war in view of ceilings on other defense spending. Despite these problems, Table 2-13 seems a plausible schedule of incremental expenditures.

Table 2-13. Peak Incremental Outlay for the War in Vietnam

Type of expenditure	Billions of current dollars
800,000 military personnel at $12,000 per man per year	9.6
250,000 civilian personnel at $10,000 per man per year	2.5
Ground, air, and naval ordnance	5.2
500 aircraft at $3 million per aircraft (average)	1.5
Replacement of land force equipment and supplies (U.S. and ARVN)	1.3
Other procurement	1.0
Construction	1.0
Transportation and petrol, oil, and lubricants	1.0
Total	23.0

Sources: *Statement of Secretary of Defense Robert S. McNamara before the Senate Armed Services Committee on the Fiscal Year 1969–73 Defense Program and 1969 Defense Budget*, U.S. Department of Defense (Jan. 22, 1968); *Statement of Secretary of Defense Clark M. Clifford: The Fiscal Year 1970–74 Defense Program and 1970 Defense Budget*, U.S. Department of Defense (Jan. 15, 1969); *U.S. Tactical Air Power Program*, Hearings before the Preparedness Investigating Subcommittee of the Senate Committee on Armed Services, 90 Cong. 2 sess. (1968). Details do not add to total because of rounding.

The Question of Deferred Baseline Requirements

Let us assume that the figure of $23.0 billion is a correct measure of the peak annual increment to the defense budget resulting from the Vietnam war, and that the peak came in fiscal 1968. The most useful way to identify a "deficit" in baseline requirements would seem to be to inflate the "required" costs of the pre-Vietnam baseline force over the past eight years, subtract actual strategic nuclear costs and the incremental costs of the war, and compare the remainder—the "required" costs of baseline general purpose forces—with actual spending on general purpose forces. Table 2-14 shows the results of this calculation and suggests that over the full period these forces have actually run above the pre-Vietnam rate, but that, taking the past five years alone, we may have a very small deferred deficit. Table 2-15 presents an alternative technique for calculating Vietnam incremental costs. The results of the two calculations are quite similar.

Table 2-14. Total Obligational Authority for the General Purpose Forces: Comparison of Actual Amounts Provided and Amounts Required To Support the Baseline Force, Fiscal Years 1964–71

Billions of current dollars

Cost item	1964	1965	1966	1967	1968	1969	1970	1971
Required cost of total baseline force	51.6	52.0	53.0	54.0	56.0	58.0	60.0	62.0
Actual cost of strategic nuclear forces[a]	17.1	14.2	14.3	14.9	16.6	19.1	17.9	18.2
Required cost of baseline general purpose forces[b]	34.5	37.8	38.7	39.1	39.4	38.9	42.1	43.8
Cost of the war in Vietnam[c]	0	0.1	6.0	18.0	23.0	22.0	17.0	11.0
Total required cost of general purpose forces	34.5	37.9	44.7	57.1	62.4	60.9	59.1	54.8
Actual cost of general purpose forces	34.5	37.3	52.2	59.6	60.3	59.6	58.3	53.4
Difference between actual and required costs	0	−0.6	+7.5	+2.4	−2.1	−1.3	−0.8	−1.4

Sources: See Tables 2-1, 2-4, 2-11, and 2-15. See also the following U.S. Department of Defense releases: *Statement of Secretary of Defense Robert S. McNamara before the Senate Armed Services Committee on the Fiscal Year 1969–73 Defense Program and 1969 Defense Budget* (Jan. 22, 1968); *Statement of Secretary of Defense Clark M. Clifford: The Fiscal Year 1970–74 Defense Program and 1970 Defense Budget* (Jan. 15, 1969); *Statement of Secretary of Defense Melvin R. Laird before a Joint Session of the Senate Armed Services Committee and the Senate Subcommittee on Department of Defense Appropriations on the Fiscal Year 1971 Defense Program and Budget* (Feb. 20, 1970).

a. Cost of the strategic forces program plus a share of intelligence and communications, research and development, and general support costs.

b. Cost of the general purpose forces program plus a share of intelligence and communications, research and development, and general support costs, plus all of airlift and sealift, National Guard and Reserve forces, and support of other nations.

c. The cost of the war in Vietnam is given in outlays rather than total obligational authority. This explains the anomalies in fiscal 1966 and fiscal 1967 when total obligational authority was running well ahead of outlays for Vietnam. The net result, however, is that total obligational authority for the general purpose forces has been $3.5 billion more than "required" during the seven years of the war.

However, a number of considerations make it likely that even this almost indiscernible deficit does not exist. First, there is nothing obligatory about the pre-Vietnam rate of expenditure for the baseline general purpose forces. What is important is not some arbitrary standard, but how well the forces would perform against potential enemies. By this measure, at least according to Secretary McNamara, the performance of the general purpose forces had improved very considerably between 1961 and 1968 (see Table 2-16), and would continue to do so with existing programs.

Finally, military forces that do not suffer a defeat on the battlefield usually find themselves in a more modern condition at the end of a war than at its beginning. The U.S. forces will inherit from Vietnam not only a great deal of equipment in the field, but also materiel that is on order and in the pipeline. To the extent that there is deferred demand, it can be met in most areas from those inventories. Nonetheless, while the Air Force has more of the newest aircraft than it would have procured under peacetime baseline programming, it has also retained more older aircraft than would have been the case without the war. There is a sense in which a similar fate has befallen the Navy. The turnover in naval aircraft has been very extensive during the past five years, but the modernization program for Navy ships has slipped—not for lack of money, but because the shipyards in most demand have been crowded with overhauls and conversions as well as new construction. The Army has acquired new helicopters, armored vehicles, tanks, and rifles. For reasons that are not entirely clear, only domestic military construction and base maintenance have probably suffered seriously as a result of the war.

Table 2-15. Estimated Manpower Requirements and Incremental Costs of the War in Vietnam, Fiscal Years 1968–72[a]

Cost items in millions of current dollars

Item	1968	1969	1970	1971	1972
Military personnel required					
In Vietnam	536,100	538,200	380,000	200,000	50,000
In line of communications and training	263,900	233,447	180,714	120,714	20,000
Civilian personnel required	250,000	227,771	167,794	111,894	10,000
Total personnel requirement	1,050,000	999,418	728,508	432,608	80,000
Cost					
In Vietnam[b]	$17,477	$17,545	$12,388	$6,520	$1,630
In line of communications and training[c]	3,167	2,801	2,169	1,449	240
Cost of civilian personnel[d]	2,500	2,278	1,678	1,119	100
Total incremental cost	$23,144	$22,624	$16,235	$9,088	$1,970

Sources: See Tables 2-7, 2-11, and 2-13. See also the sources for Table 2-14.

a. The manpower data in this table are end-of-year figures, and the costs developed from them represent annual rates of outlays at year end. The techniques used to estimate incremental costs—the application of cost factors to manpower numbers—give results which are basically consistent in level and trend, although not precisely the same as the Vietnam costs shown in Table 2-14.

b. $32,600 per man per year, based on an average annual rate of $12,000 per man for pay and allowances, and average annual combat costs per man of $20,600. Combat costs in fiscal 1968 were taken to be $11.0 billion, allocated as follows: ground, air, and naval ordnance, $5.2 billion; replacement aircraft (500 at $3 million each), $1.5 billion; replacement of land force equipment and supplies, both U.S. and ARVN, $1.3 billion; other procurement, $1.0 billion; construction, $1.0 billion; and transportation and petrol, oil, and lubricants, $1.0 billion. The $11.0 billion total divided by 536,100 men yields $20,600 per man.

c. $12,000 per man per year.

d. $10,000 per man per year.

Table 2-16. Capabilities of General Purpose Forces at the End of Fiscal Year 1968

Force element or characteristic	Index of effectiveness (1961 = 100)[a]
Army artillery	
Authorized number of pieces	179
Sustained-fire salvo rate	185
Sustained-fire lethal-area rate	175
Army medium and light tanks	
Authorized number	95
Total range	188
Total salvo capacity	139
Total lethal-area capacity	181
Army cargo trucks and trailers	
Authorized number[b]	164
Dry-cargo lift capacity[c]	182
Liquid-cargo lift capacity[d]	225
Tactical aircraft payload capability	213[e]
Airborne ASW search capability	231
ASW escort (screen) capability	163
Fleet AAW capability:	
Total number of missile ships[f]	326
Number of missile ships with Navy tactical data system[g]	750
Amphibious assault capability:	
Total number of amphibious assault ships[h]	137
Number of fast, modern amphibious assault ships[i]	238
Total lift capacity	130
Fast lift capacity	290

Source: *Statement of Secretary of Defense Robert S. McNamara before the Senate Armed Services Committee on the Fiscal Year 1969–73 Defense Program and 1969 Defense Budget*, U.S. Department of Defense (Jan. 22, 1968), pp. 88–94.

a. Index of effectiveness is defined as the ratio, multiplied by 100, of the value of the force element or characteristic at the end of fiscal 1968 to its value at the end of fiscal 1961, with the exception stated in note (e) below.

b. Actual numbers, in thousands, were as follows: 271.5 at end of fiscal 1961; 444.6 at end of fiscal 1968.

c. Actual lift capacities, in thousands of tons, were as follows: 437.3 at end of fiscal 1961; 797.0 at end of fiscal 1968.

d. Actual lift capacities, in millions of gallons, were as follows: 15.5 at end of fiscal 1961; 34.7 at end of fiscal 1968.

e. Computed as of the end of fiscal 1967, rather than fiscal 1968.

f. Actual numbers were as follows: 23 at end of fiscal 1961; 75 at end of fiscal 1968.

g. Actual numbers were as follows: 2 at end of fiscal 1961; 15 at end of fiscal 1968.

h. Actual numbers were as follows: 104 at end of fiscal 1961; 142 at end of fiscal 1968.

i. Actual numbers were as follows: 13 at end of fiscal 1961; 31 at end of fiscal 1968.

In summary, a case can be made that there is some deferred demand, but it seems to be of a very modest character and is being met as Vietnam spending declines. If forces are actually reduced below the pre-Vietnam baseline after the war and the older equipment and bases are phased out, the remaining capabilities should be very modern indeed.

Conclusion

For many citizens the decline in defense spending in 1971 will come not only as a welcome relief, but also as a signal of an impending shift in national priorities. This review has sought to demonstrate that this is not a necessary conclusion from the evidence in the budget estimates and associated narrative. Indeed, it is worth remembering that although defense expenditures have fluctuated as a percentage of the gross national product over the past thirty years, they have consistently risen in absolute terms after each war (see Table 2-17). Given

Table 2-17. Military Outlays in Interwar Years in Current and Constant Dollars, Fiscal Years 1939–60

Dollar items in billions

Fiscal year	Gross national product, current dollars	Military outlays		Deflator (1964 = 100)	Military outlays, 1964 dollars
		Amount, current dollars	Percentage of GNP		
1939	87.6	1.2	1.3	36.4	3.2
1940	95.0	1.6	1.6	35.8	4.4
Second World War . . . .
1947	219.8	13.8	6.3	58.5	23.6
1948	243.5	11.1	4.6	62.2	17.8
1949	260.0	12.0	4.6	65.1	18.4
1950	263.3	11.9	4.5	65.0	18.4
Korean conflict ·
1955	378.6	37.4	9.9	77.5	48.2
1956	409.4	37.7	9.2	81.7	46.2
1957	431.3	40.2	9.3	85.4	47.1
1958	440.3	41.4	9.4	89.1	46.5
1959	469.1	43.7	9.3	91.1	48.0
1960	495.2	43.1	8.7	92.9	46.4

Source: Testimony of Robert C. Moot in *The Military Budget and National Economic Priorities*, Hearings before the Subcommittee on Economy in Government of the Joint Economic Committee, 91 Cong. 1 sess. (1969), Part 1, pp. 374–75.

this tendency, there is no reason to expect the trend automatically to be different when the Vietnam conflict is over. To reverse the trend, if that is desirable, will require a major conscious effort not only by public officials but by the body politic as well.

There is no escaping the fact that the making of a defense budget demands difficult and fundamental choices. Simplistic theories about defense outlays are inadequate to the depth of security interests and the complexity of the means employed to protect them. They miss the central point that there is a hierarchy of decisions along the way to the defense budget and that each step confronts the President with a variety of complicated issues as he struggles with even broader questions of allocating federal funds. Only by addressing these steps in a serious and knowledgeable way can those not burdened with his responsibilities be helpful.

3. Health, Education, and Income Maintenance

BUDGET ISSUES in health, education, and income maintenance are closely intertwined. Most of these programs are administered by the Department of Health, Education, and Welfare (HEW), the government's largest civilian agency. When funds are tight, there is a tendency to assign budgetary targets to individual agencies, reflecting not only program priorities but also the attempt to keep increases in any one department from getting out of line. Hence, increases in one part of HEW may lead to cuts in others. More important, many of these programs are directed at the same problem: the alleviation of poverty. With limited funds, difficult choices must be made among alternative strategies for reducing poverty. Should funds be used to increase the incomes of the poor directly through income maintenance programs, or to provide them with health, education, and other services, or should funds be invested in future improvements in health and education for the poor and everyone else?

In 1971 the proposed budget for HEW grows by 13 percent over 1970 and by 28 percent over 1969—a faster rate than for any other agency. But the largest part of the increase reflects growth in expenditures not subject to immediate budgetary control. Of the $7.0 billion rise in HEW expenditures between 1970 and 1971, $5.9 billion reflects increased outlays for social security, Medicare, Medicaid, and public assistance. An additional $500 million is the estimated 1971 cost of the proposed family assistance plan.

Table 3-1. Budget Obligations of the Department of Health, Education, and Welfare, Various Fiscal Years, 1955–71 [a]

Millions of dollars

Program	1955	1960	1965	1967	1968	1969	1970 estimate	1971 estimate
Total	**6,458**	**14,588**	**24,209**	**38,298**	**45,122**	**50,492**	**56,888**	**64,491**
Social Security Administration	**4,414**	**10,984**	**16,950**	**26,958**	**31,324**	**36,036**	**41,366**	**46,888**
Old-Age, Survivors, and Disability Insurance	4,414	10,981	16,944	22,495	24,413	27,780	31,911	35,449
Medicare	…	…	…	4,456	6,903	8,248	9,426	11,268
Regular budget total (excluding Social Security Administration)	**2,044**	**3,604**	**7,259**	**11,340**	**13,798**	**14,455**	**15,522**	**17,603**
Major uncontrollable programs	**1,402**	**2,094**	**3,257**	**4,218**	**5,733**	**6,231**	**7,524**	**8,989**
Public assistance	1,402	2,094	2,966	3,032	3,588	3,955	4,697	6,111
Medicaid	…	…	290	1,187	2,145	2,275	2,827	2,879
Health programs (excluding Medicare and Medicaid)	**288**	**933**	**2,280**	**2,865**	**3,418**	**3,587**	**3,594**	**3,703**
Research	87	372	947	1,146	1,123	1,109	1,072	1,183
Service	118	224	479	728	793	1,019	1,031	1,139
Training	11	90	357	541	940	962	938	899
Construction (care facilities)	62	161	264	299	350	289	309	196
Consumer protection	9	86	233	151	211	207	244	286
Health programs (including Medicare and Medicaid) [b]	**(288)**	**(933)**	**(2,571)**	**(8,508)**	**(12,466)**	**(14,111)**	**(15,847)**	**(17,850)**
Education	**302**	**470**	**1,498**	**3,705**	**4,008**	**3,829**	**3,370**	**3,738**
Elementary and secondary education	286	381	748	2,328	2,558	2,468	1,994	2,333
Impacted areas	256	254	408	445	502	559	201	425
Disadvantaged children	…	…	…	1,053	1,187	1,123	1,226	1,300
Vocational education	30	47	168	266	265	255	270	279
Categorical aid	…	81	172	565	604	531	296	309
Higher education	5	58	585	1,023	1,054	880	837	813
Research and training	…	6	112	276	301	386	408	456
Social and rehabilitation services (excluding public assistance)	**44**	**90**	**198**	**498**	**569**	**717**	**919**	**1,046**
Work Incentive Program (WIN)	…	…	…	…	10	115	130	170
Vocational rehabilitation	25	50	97	256	307	375	514	536
Research and training	1	25	68	110	114	138	156	186

Source: Compiled from *The Budget of the United States Government . . . Appendix*, for Fiscal Years 1957, 1962, 1967, 1969, 1970, and 1971. The 1970 figures are from the 1971 budget document and are not the same as those provided in the final appropriations act for fiscal 1970. Figures are rounded and may not add to totals.

a. The total and most of the subtotals include items not shown separately.
b. Entries are the sums of separate entries above.

To clarify the choices reflected in the 1971 budget, this section first reviews briefly the history of federal involvement in health, education, and income maintenance. Next, several budget alternatives and decisions are examined, and finally some basic issues cutting across program lines are discussed.

The Legacy of 1935–70

The current mix of HEW programs was developed over a span of three decades, beginning with the social security and public assistance programs of the mid-1930s and culminating in the enactment of dozens of categorical grant programs in the 1960s. Each of these bursts of legislative achievement left its imprint on the 1971 budget. In fact, the President's budget reflects only one important new legislative departure: the welfare reform, or family assistance program. Otherwise it is mainly a continuation of existing programs, each scaled to the present fiscal situation and to the spending priorities asserted by the President.

To understand the proposed budget for HEW therefore requires an awareness of past decisions. The growth and change in departmental programs since 1955 are shown in Table 3-1 and are discussed briefly below.

Helping certain individuals to maintain their income in the face of adversity became a federal responsibility in the 1930s. The social security system has been designed to protect against devastating loss of family income due to death, disability, or retirement. Public assistance was designed to help certain people—the blind, the aged, mothers with dependent children, and the disabled—whose minimum needs were not met by personal income or social insurance.

These programs constituted the core of the HEW budget when the department was formed in 1953. Of a $6.5 billion budget in 1955, social security and public assistance accounted for $5.7 billion. Health programs amounted to less than $300 million, or less than 2 percent of the nation's total health expenditures. Education programs amounted to slightly more than $300 million, or about 2 percent of national education expenditures. Only three of today's education programs existed in 1955. Assistance to "impacted areas" began as an emergency program for school districts burdened by military installations in the Korean war. Aid to vocational education and land grant colleges had longer histories but accounted for small sums in 1955. The federal presence in education, as in health, was negligible.

Income maintenance expenditures continued to grow in the 1960s. Social security beneficiaries increased in number and benefit levels were raised. Public assistance recipients also increased and received higher payments. But the most dramatic growth occurred in other areas. Dozens of new programs were added and, for the first time, health, education, and social services became important areas of federal activity.

The federal role in education began to change in the aftermath of Sputnik. One manifestation of the shift was the passage in 1958 of the National Defense Education Act, a hodgepodge of categorical aids for instructional equipment in science and other subjects, language instruction, guidance and testing, student loans, and graduate fellowships.

In 1963 the Congress passed the Higher Education Facilities Act, providing funds for construction of college and university buildings, and in 1965 it enacted the comprehensive Elementary and Secondary Education Act (ESEA) and the Higher Education Act (HEA). Title I of ESEA authorized over $1 billion annually for aid to local school districts with high concentrations of children from low income families. Other titles provided for a variety of categorical support programs, such as library resources, textbooks, and supplementary educational services. The Higher Education Act, including later amendments, provided comprehensive programs of student aid both for needy students (grants, direct loans, work-study aid) and for others (the guaranteed bank loan program). HEA began new programs to aid teacher training, to strengthen developing (largely Negro) colleges, and to support purchases of equipment. These landmark acts had a massive impact on the federal education budget. By 1968, the budget for the Office of Education approached $4 billion, most of which represented funding of newly established programs, though older programs (vocational education and aid to impacted areas) had also grown substantially.

Health programs expanded rapidly in number and funding in the same period. Construction of health facilities under the Hill-Burton program and training of medical personnel increased, but the most spectacular growth was in outlays for health research. Funds for research more than doubled between 1960 and 1965 as extensive biomedical research programs were undertaken by the National Institutes of Health. In 1965 two titles were added to the Social Security Act and a new federal role in health was established. Title XVIII (Medicare) provided hospital and medical insurance coverage to elderly recipients of social security. Title XIX (Medicaid) provided federal funds for state programs to cover the cost of medical care for the poor and the "medically indigent"—persons who, while not poor, would have difficulty paying heavy medical bills. Outlays under both programs expanded rapidly—much more rapidly than anticipated. Between 1965 and 1968 the total health programs of HEW grew from $2.6 billion to $12.5 billion, or from 7 percent to 24 percent of national health expenditures.

Another area of budgetary growth in the mid-1960s was social services. The mystifying rise in public assistance case loads in the face of prosperity led to attempts to reduce dependency by providing services to the poor. Manpower training, vocational rehabilitation, and child welfare services all grew rapidly.

After 1967, war and inflation changed the budget picture and put severe constraints on domestic spending. In HEW, the budgetary crunch had unbalanced consequences because of the dominant position of the social security trust funds and "uncontrollable" outlays for public assistance, Medicaid, and social services. Although social security outlays (including Medicare) are financed by special taxes and are outside the regular HEW budget, their impact on HEW budgetary decisions was formidable. In 1967–69, social security outlays rose substantially because of the new Medicare program and increases in benefits designed to compensate beneficiaries for advances in the cost of living. Public assistance, Medicaid, and some social services also have a relatively uncontrollable impact on the budget; funds spent by states on these programs must be matched by the federal government in accordance with formulas prescribed in the law.

In the late 1960s, public assistance outlays climbed rapidly for a combination of reasons that are still not well understood. Increases in coverage and payment levels of state programs, migration of the poor into states with more generous programs, family instability, and increasing awareness on the part of the poor of their right to assistance, probably all contributed. Outlays under the new Medicaid program also rose rapidly. Since it seemed unconscionable to cut back on payments going directly to the neediest Americans—the freeze on welfare payments voted by the Congress was never put into effect—strenuous efforts were made to hold the line or to cut back on other programs to offset the fiscal effects of the "uncontrollables."

Planning a coherent strategy for even the "controllable" programs became extremely difficult. By the close of the 1960s, HEW was administering dozens of specific categorical programs, each of which had developed a supporting clientele on Capitol Hill and in the field. Vocational educators lobbied hard for aid to vocational education, librarians organized to increase aid to libraries, manufacturers of instructional equipment extolled the benefits of equipment programs, hospital associations fought for hospital construction money, and so forth.

To be sure, doubts had arisen about the effectiveness of many of these programs. The multiplicity of categories led to red tape and high administrative costs, and the programs did not always meet the most urgent local needs. Moreover, some programs were proving ill adapted to new priorities. Under the state-administered Hill-Burton program, hospital construction was concentrated in small towns and rural areas rather than in larger cities, where needs for modernization and expansion of hospitals were mounting rapidly. The impacted aid program had become one of general assistance to districts with large numbers of children of federal employees. Its disbursements bore little relation to any indicator of educational need. In 1969, for example, the program conferred on three wealthy suburban counties around Washington, D.C., five times the aid received by New York City, and on Brevard County, Florida, a little more aid than on Chicago or Philadelphia. (See Chapter 5.)

In 1968 and 1969, the growth of education and health programs (except Medicare and Medicaid) virtually ceased, despite rising costs. Construction of hospitals and college buildings was delayed and several shifts were made from grant to loan financing to get programs "off the budget."

1970: The Administration versus the Congress

The HEW budget dilemma at the end of the 1960s could be summarized as follows:

1. Strong efforts were being made to reduce the rate of growth of the total budget in the face of war and inflation.

2. Uncontrollable expenditures for social security, public assistance, Medicare, Medicaid, and social services were rising faster than the total budget. Most of these expenditures went directly to the neediest Americans, and the Department of Health, Education, and Welfare had neither the authority nor the desire to reduce them.

3. To hold the budget within tolerable limits and to make a little room for new priorities, it would be necessary to cut into existing programs. Doubts had arisen about the effectiveness of many existing categorical aid programs and about the sheer number of special categories. Nevertheless, each category had its supporters, and the least effective programs sometimes seemed the hardest to cut.

The big question facing the incoming administration was the same one that had faced the previous administration: Could some way be found to reorient the HEW budget toward new priorities at a time when its total growth was severely limited? The Nixon administration's budget for 1970 presented to the Congress in April 1969 made drastic cuts in several existing programs; some of the resultant savings were programmed for the expansion of high priority efforts, and the remainder were to be used to help achieve overall budget economies.

In education, the administration sharply reduced the impacted aid program; consolidated and reduced several categorical programs for school library resources, guidance and counseling, and equipment and remodeling; reduced college construction grants and direct loans to students; and reduced funds for libraries. Education funds were added for assisting disadvantaged children (Title I of ESEA and dropout prevention) and for grants to needy college students. Emphasis was placed on programs to develop new knowledge about educational effectiveness. Money was added for evaluation and for a new program of experimental schools. The additions were not as large as the cuts, however. In order to meet overall expenditure objectives, the administration's total budget for the Office of Education was about $450 million below the 1969 level. The long-term reordering of priorities for federal support of education thus became associated in many minds with a more temporary objective—a reduction in total support.

In health, the administration's budget also attempted to reorder priorities, albeit less drastically than in education, by cutting Hill-Burton hospital construction and increasing funds for formula grants to states, regional medical programs, migrant health, and mental health centers.

The big cuts in education were a ready-made issue for the opposition and an open invitation to lobbying efforts on the part of those whose programs were slashed. Traditionally independent factions of educators, supply industries, and professional associations worked together on an alternative to the administration's budget. They lobbied for more funds for impacted aid, the categorical programs, vocational education, college construction, and library programs.

In January 1970, the Congress passed a $17.7 billion appropriation for health, education, and welfare, restoring most of the cuts proposed by the President and increasing some of his "low priority" programs above the previous year's spending level. This bill was vetoed by President Nixon on grounds that the increased appropriations were inflationary and that the added funds were for low priority programs. Following failure of the House to override the veto and several weeks of public debate and backstage negotiation, the Congress approved and the President signed a $17 billion compromise measure (the actual amount appropriated was approximately $300 million higher, but the Congress directed the President to reduce authorized spending by 2 percent). This amount is $700 million below the vetoed appropriation but still $550 million above the spending level proposed by the President in April 1969. (See Table 3-2.)

The Congress not only voted more funds for education than the administration requested, but also reversed administration priorities. Programs to which the administration had given low priority received major increases and the administration's request for experimental schools was denied. Impacted aid, which the President had specifically criticized, was restored to its 1969 level. In health, Hill-Burton funds were increased above the President's request. The net result of congressional action was that the 1970 education budget was more in line with the 1969 budget than with the President's 1970 budget request.

1971: Major Alternatives and Decisions

This section does not attempt to consider the whole range of HEW budget alternatives. Rather it focuses on four major problem areas in which the administration had definite options. It describes the problems, reviews the feasible options, and discusses the choices made in the 1971 budget.

Table 3-2. Appropriations for the Department of Health, Education, and Welfare, by Program, Fiscal Year 1969, and Amounts Requested, Vetoed, and Enacted, Fiscal Year 1970[a]

Millions of dollars

Program	1969 actual	1970 requested	1970 vetoed	1970 enacted[b]
Total	**15,457**	**16,474**	**17,736**	**17,023**
Health	**2,714**	**2,712**	**2,947**	**2,725**
National Institutes of Health	1,395	1,449	1,546	1,436
Health Services and Mental Health Administration[c]	819	877	896	874
Hospital construction	258	154	258	176
Consumer protection	227	229	243	236
Other	15	3	3	3
Education	**3,647**	**3,198**	**4,276**	**3,814**
Elementary and secondary education				
Impacted areas	521	202	600	521
Disadvantaged children	1,136	1,260	1,427	1,365
Vocational education	248	279	489	368
Categorical aid	340	155	301	205
Higher education				
Direct loans	193	162	229	196
Construction grants	91	43	76	71
Research and training	203	242	215	201
Other	915	855	939	887
Social and rehabilitation services	**7,338**	**8,451**	**8,401**	**8,371**
Public assistance	6,416	7,351	7,352	7,352
Work Incentive Program (WIN)	118	130	120	102
Vocational rehabilitation	369	500	465	464
Other	435	470	464	453
Other	**1,758**	**2,113**	**2,112**	**2,112**

Source: First three columns: U.S. Department of Health, Education, and Welfare, "Congressional Action on the 1970 HEW-Labor Appropriation Bill" (Feb. 20, 1970; processed). Last column: *Congressional Record*, daily ed., March 4, 1970, pp. S 2915–S 2930. Figures are rounded and may not add to totals.

a. Excluding trust funds.

b. Reflects HEW allocation of 2 percent reduction from 1970 appropriations required by Sec. 410 of the appropriations act.

c. Excluding hospital construction.

The budget appears to accord relatively high priority to HEW programs as a whole, inasmuch as total spending by HEW rises $7 billion above the 1970 level. However, the increases are highly uneven. Social security increases account for $5.1 billion, of which $1.2 billion is for Medicare. Public assistance and Medicaid account for $800 million. The "controllable" health programs rise hardly at all. Education is again accorded low priority. The same strategy used in fiscal 1970 is reflected in 1971: cutting the low priority education programs drastically to make room for expansion in other programs. Indeed the proposed appropriations for the 1971 education budget are lower than in 1969 and below the 1970 budget approved by the Congress after the 1971 budget was submitted. In view of this fact, it seems possible that the administration will later increase the education budget, raising some of the programs closer to the levels voted by the Congress for 1970. The President has already stated his intention to increase his earlier 1971 appropriations request for certain items in elementary and secondary education, in connection with the "Right to Read" program; but even with these increases, the total for the affected items would remain below the 1970 level.

Welfare Reform

Perhaps the most difficult question facing the administration in the HEW area was what to do about welfare. The public assistance system was working badly and almost everyone was dissatisfied with it—those who administered it, those who paid for it, and even those who received its benefits.

Public assistance is not a general system of aid to the needy. It was originally set up to help certain categories of needy people who were thought to be unable to work and who were not adequately covered by social insurance. The federal government matches state payments to the aged, to the permanently and totally disabled, to the blind, and to families with dependent children (AFDC). AFDC is basically a program for mothers with children and no male breadwinner. Recent amendments allow the states to make payments to families with unemployed fathers, but less than half the states have chosen to do so.

This patchwork of programs has been subject to major criticism. Benefit levels are inadequate, especially in the poorest states, and wide disparities in payment levels exist among states and among different categories of aid recipients. Benefits under AFDC usually are lower in relation to need than are those for the adult categories (aged, blind, disabled). Many needy persons are not eligible; although about one-third of the poor are in families headed by a working male, such families are ineligible for federal assistance. This exclusion increases incentives for fathers to desert their families. Administration of the program often has been confusing and embarrassing to the recipient. Finally, rising case loads have placed a heavy financial burden on state and local governments, especially those of major cities, in which a large portion of the poor now live.

The administration decided quickly that something must be done to reform the welfare system. However, barring a major increase in budgetary resources, it could not give serious consideration to drastic solutions, some of which would cost as much as $10 billion to $20 billion annually. The problem facing the administration was to design a workable reform that would answer the above criticisms by (1) raising income levels for the neediest families, (2) reducing disparities among states and different types of poor people, (3) increasing incentives to work and to keep families together, and (4) relieving the states of part of the burden. Moreover, given the budget constraints in 1971 and immediately following years, a ceiling of roughly $5 billion would have to be set for the added costs of the reform program in its first full year of operation.

Several approaches were possible. One was to retain but improve the existing welfare system by raising the federal share of welfare costs, requiring a minimum level of benefits under state welfare payments, making aid to families with unemployed fathers mandatory, and extending federal support for emergency assistance. Such incremental reforms clearly have merits. Nevertheless, patching up the existing system would do nothing to improve the discredited image of the welfare program or to move toward a more general system of aid to all the needy, including the working poor.

Some favored moving away from AFDC to a general children's allowance with payments for all children regardless of family income level. This option was ruled out because most children are not poor and aiding all children is an exceedingly expensive way of reaching poor children. A $5 billion children's allowance would not provide even minimum support for the needy.

The final decision was a compromise. In programs for the aged, blind, and disabled poor, the existing welfare system was retained with a new federal minimum and higher federal matching contributions. For families with children, however, the administration proposed that the federal government withdraw entirely from the present AFDC program and substitute a new family assistance program with uniform federal standards of eligibility and payment. Under the family assistance plan, a family of four with no other earnings would receive an annual payment of $1,600. In addition these families would be allowed to keep the first $720 of earnings without a reduction in their basic payment, and 50 cents out of each dollar earned thereafter.

The family assistance plan would raise payment levels for persons already on welfare in the poorest southern states. More significantly, however, it would extend aid to the working poor in all states, adding perhaps 10 million persons to the assistance rolls. In most states, however, families eligible for assistance already receive more than the proposed new federal minimum. These states would be required to retain supplementary programs for those currently eligible and to pay the costs of these programs.

In addition to the proposed reforms in cash welfare payments, the budget calls for a substantial expansion of the food stamp program to all areas of the country. The program provides low-income families with stamps that can be redeemed for food, and charges them substantially less than the stamps are worth. The food stamp subsidy, combined with family assistance, would bring the basic federal guarantee to a family of four with no other earnings to $2,464 a year. An all-cash program, rather than a combination of cash and food stamps, would be simpler to administer and would give recipients more freedom in spending their income. However, given strong interests in food stamps among both agricultural groups and antihunger crusaders, the combined plan was chosen. The cost of the first full year of the family assistance plan is estimated to be about $4.4 billion. Including the larger food stamp programs, the total additional cost of the welfare reform would be about $5.2 billion in the first full year. The 1971 budget assumes, however, that the family assistance plan will not get under way until late in the year. It includes $500 million for family assistance and an increase of $764 million for food stamps and related nutrition programs.

One of the administration's main objectives in devising the family assistance plan was to provide greater work incentives for welfare recipients. And it does improve upon the existing system. The potential success of the plan is threatened, however, by the way in which it combines with the food stamp and certain other subsidy programs to reduce substantially the fraction of earned income that subsidy recipients may keep. Under the family assistance program, half of all earnings above the first $720 a year will be applied to reduce the subsidy payment. For every dollar of additional income, including welfare payments, the value of food stamps provided to recipients will be cut roughly 30 cents for most recipients. In addition there is a 5 percent social security tax on earnings. Taken together, these features of federal programs mean that welfare recipients will have to give up 70 percent of any earnings over and above the first $720 a year. Moreover, those who receive some form of housing subsidy will have an additional percentage of their earnings offset by a reduction in the value of that subsidy. Consequently, many welfare recipients will be able to retain only a very small fraction of the rewards from productive work and will have little monetary incentive to seek such work.

One of the difficulties caused by the series of piecemeal welfare and subsidy payments is this unintended effect on subsidy recipients. It should not be impossible, however, to devise statutory language and administrative procedures that would set a limit on the percentage of earnings that would be "taxed" away by the combined application of various subsidy formulas.

Elementary and Secondary Education

In drafting its elementary and secondary education budget, the administration was confronted with the two basic problems of American education:

The fiscal mismatch: the resources to support education are not located where the needs are greatest. Disparities among states in expenditures per student are very large. The lower-income states, especially those of the South, have few resources to spend on education even when their tax effort is substantial. But inequalities *within* states are also great and of increasing concern. Schools in big cities need larger expenditures per student than those elsewhere because of heavy concentrations of poor children with exceptional needs, and high costs of land and teachers. Yet the capacity of large cities to raise additional funds for education has eroded as wealthier citizens and industry have moved to the suburbs and as noneducation costs have risen.

The quality problem: schools are not as effective as they could be. Americans seem to be experiencing a crisis of confidence in their schools. Statistical studies such as the Coleman report indicate clearly that low-income children, on the average, show relatively low achievement in school. According to the commissioner of education, more than 10 million youngsters have significant reading difficulties. Dissatisfaction with the schools is not confined, however, to the problems of reading deficiencies or under-achievement of low-income youngsters. Student unrest and the growing use of drugs are seen by many as evidence of the failure of the schools to motivate students of all income levels.

The administration's strategy for education seems to rest on the following positions:

REDIRECTING EXISTING PROGRAMS. The budget gives repeated emphasis to redirecting existing programs. For example, in the program of grants to the states for supplementary services, "States will be encouraged to use these grants to fund . . . the 'Right to Read' program." In the impacted areas program, "proposed legislation will . . . concentrate payments" on those districts where legitimate fiscal needs can be discerned. In vocational education, states "will be encouraged to use more . . . for disadvantaged students." Emphasis in the research budget will be shifted to innovative projects under the proposed experimental schools program.

These positions were strongly supported in the President's message on education, sent to the Congress on March 3. The President urged that the 1970s "mark the beginning of an era of reform and progress" in education. He called for "thoughtful redirection to improve our ability to make up for environmental deficiencies among the poor, . . . more efficient use of the dollars spent on education, . . . [and] structural reforms to accommodate new discoveries."

These promised new departures are certain to provoke political and bureaucratic struggles. Moreover, to reallocate funds within the education budget, without enlarging the total, means withdrawing support from some activities already receiving funds. This is precisely the approach that was encouraged in the President's 1970 education budget, and it led to the creation of a powerful education lobby and to the near-stalemate on education appropriations. Moreover, in many of the programs that the administration will attempt to redirect, the power of the federal government is severely limited because the states determine the projects to be supported.

RESEARCH AND EXPERIMENTATION. The keystone of the administration's education strategy is research to improve the quality and effectiveness of education and experimentation with new educational techniques and structures. In his education message, the President proposed the establishment of a national institute of education "to evaluate new departures in teaching." The institute would focus on compensatory programs for poor children, improvement of reading, the use of television to foster out-of-school learning, and the development of experimental schools. The message proposed a $250 million level of support for the institute "when fully developed," $52 million for preschool child development projects, and substantially higher spending on research and training.

EQUALIZATION. At least for fiscal year 1971, no significant attempt is made to use federal aid to equalize education spending among school districts. Title I aid, the main redistributive program in the budget, is set at $1.3 billion for 1971, slightly less than the amount appropriated for 1970. In almost all the other support programs for elementary and secondary education, the administration's 1971 request is well below the amounts finally appropriated for 1970. The administration did not seek new legislation and financing for an urban education act, as recommended by an HEW task force, nor did it propose full funding of Title I of ESEA. Either of these strategies would have been very expensive. To provide $300 per pupil in each city with over 100,000 population would cost $3.5 billion. The full funding of Title I, which is based on the number of children from families who have incomes under $3,000 or who are on welfare or in institutions, would cost $2.5 billion, double the fiscal 1969 appropriation.

FUTURE AID TO EDUCATION. Two weeks after the budget message was submitted to the Congress, the commissioner of education promised "substantial increases in federal aid to education . . . when we have taken steps to put ourselves in a better position to assure maximum results."[1] Presumably, the research and experimentation advocated in the education message are to pave the way for future advances in financial support. "To chart the fiscal course . . . for the seventies," the President established a President's Commission on School Finance to report on future needs and priorities.

In summary, the 1971 budget and education messages recognize the central problems facing elementary and secondary education. For the short run, few substantial changes are proposed. But by attempting to focus existing programs on central problems and by creating new bodies to study and direct research in the quality and financing of schools, the administration hopes to assure more productive use of present federal funds. On the assumption that these efforts will succeed, there have been more or less explicit hints of larger amounts for these programs in the future.

Higher Education

The Nixon administration inherited a broad collection of federal legislation authorizing support for higher education. There are programs of support for relatively low-income students (grants, work-study, and subsidized loans), for middle- and upper-income students (partly subsidized bank loans), for construction of college buildings (grants, loans, and subsidies for loans), for graduate student support, for international studies, for land grant colleges, for developing colleges (predominantly black), and for equipment and library materials. Most of these programs were established in the early and mid-1960s. After growing rapidly for several years, appropriations began to level off under the Vietnam budget squeeze in the late 1960s. As a theme for the federal role in higher education, the Johnson administration decided in its closing years that budgetary priority should be given to support for students, as opposed to institutional, general purpose, or categorical grants. The new administration has continued this strategy, though with relatively little increase in financial support.

Several alternative proposals for higher education received attention during 1969.

1. *Student aid.* The administration was urged to expand existing programs of aid for low-income students so as to achieve more equitable educational opportunity in higher education. But proposals involving substantial increases in grants to poor students appeared to be unpopular in the Congress.

2. *Community colleges.* HEW Secretary Finch suggested a new program of support for junior and community colleges. He regarded community colleges as an important hope for the future and urged the development of innovative programs in this sector of post-secondary education. Plans for the support of community colleges were drafted in the administration and others were introduced in the Congress.

3. *Educational reform.* As student unrest became widespread, proposals were advanced for federal participation in the reform of higher education through sponsorship of innovative approaches to learning. Several ambitious programs were drafted for this purpose.

4. *Institutional grants.* A program of "formula institutional aid" has been approved several times by a House committee concerned with science education, but the concept of general institutional aid has never won the support of any administration.

In summary, the 1971 budget proposals on higher education are very much a holding operation, reproducing the past with a few minor changes. In the student aid programs, there will be a small increase in the number of students receiving grants and a proportionately larger reduction in those receiving college-administered loans under the National Defense Education Act (NDEA). Substantial growth is anticipated in the program of guaranteed bank loans, and over 1 million students—an increase of about 15 percent from the prior year—are expected to participate. Compared with the college-administered programs, this program serves a higher-income clientele, and these actions would therefore indicate a shift in support towards middle- and upper-income college students in the 1971 budget. At the same time, however, the administration has proposed a 50 percent expansion in project grants supporting special programs for disadvantaged students in college.

Almost all forms of assistance to educational institutions (as opposed to direct aid to students) are cut back in the 1971 budget. Support for language training and area studies is substantially reduced. Annual aid to land grant colleges is eliminated. Construction grants are reduced to zero from over $200 million two years ago. The number of NDEA graduate fellowships and the allied institutional support funded under this program are reduced to barely half the 1968 level. The only budget increases are for a new interest subsidy for college construction to take the place of construction grants and a small increase for aid to developing colleges—just enough to replace the support they would lose under the reduction in aid to land grant colleges.

All the constraints on the HEW budget seem to have pressed on higher education in 1971. The growth in public assistance, Medicaid, and social security have held down the total education budget. Within education, the administration has made more commitments and faces stronger congressional and public pressures in elementary and secondary education than in higher education. Within higher education, the guaranteed bank loan program is an uncontrollable of sorts. Money must be set aside to provide interest payments for these loans (in fiscal 1971, this uncontrollable increase in obligations will amount to some $35 million). In 1970, the administration attempted to enlarge grant support for low-income students, but the Congress made substantial cuts in these requests. What appears to be acceptable to the Congress is expansion in construction grant programs and in college-based student loan programs, neither of which ranks high in the administration's set of priorities.

In mid-March, the administration sent the Congress a message on higher education. It proposes a complete revamping of the student aid programs effective in fiscal 1972; thereafter, subsidized loans, grants, and work programs would be available only to students from families with incomes of less than $10,000. A national student loan association would provide a larger supply of funds for an unsubsidized student loan program open to all students. The message recommends a small program of career education to assist states in meeting the costs of specialized vocational programs, particularly in community colleges. It also calls for the establishment of a national foundation on higher education to provide project grants to support "new ideas and reform in higher education" and to provide "an organization concerned . . . with the development of national policy in higher education."

The Medical Price Problem

For the last several years medical fees have been rising about 6 percent a year and hospital charges about twice that fast. Price rises of this magnitude not only cause hardship to individuals who must purchase medical care but also lead to rapid escalation in the cost of government medical care programs, especially Medicare and Medicaid. The basic reasons for the rapid increase in these prices are the pressure of rising demand for services on a relatively fixed supply and the lack of incentives to use medical resources efficiently.

The demand for medical care has been rising for a variety of reasons. Population and per capita utilization of medical services have been growing. Medicare and Medicaid have exerted pressure by sharply expanding the ability of the old and the poor to purchase medical care. The overall supply of doctors and health facilities has grown slowly and not always where it was most needed. Perhaps the most serious problem is that the large medical bills are now paid by third parties—Medicare, Medicaid, and private insurance—and the providers of service encounter less price resistance by users. In fact the systems of payment encourage the use of expensive hospital care, when many cases could be cared for just as adequately but less expensively at home or in ambulatory or outpatient facilities. There is some evidence that medical plans under which subscribers prepay a single fee for comprehensive care tend to reduce the excessive use of hospitals.

These problems suggest four major options: (1) Permit Medicare and Medicaid costs to continue to rise with prices. (2) Reduce the pressure of demand as well as the cost to the federal government by cutting coverage or benefits under Medicare or Medicaid. This would mean cutting service to patients unless states or localities picked up the slack. (3) Hold down the costs of Medicare or Medicaid without reducing service levels by introducing fee schedules or incentives for more efficient delivery of services. (4) Take steps to increase the supply of medical services in the longer run and to use the supply more efficiently. These steps could include training more physicians and ancillary personnel and expanding health facilities, especially lower-cost ambulatory outpatient and extended care facilities.

The 1971 budget suggests that the course chosen is a combination of the last three approaches. Medicare benefits were not cut back, but the price to the beneficiaries of the supplementary medical insurance was increased to cover rising costs. In addition, the administration has made clear that to hold prices down, it is seriously considering drastic alterations in the reimbursement mechanism under Medicare. It proposes to encourage the use of prepayment plans for comprehensive medical care, the negotiation of hospital payments in advance, and the introduction of an index of physicians' costs as a measure of the justified rate of reimbursement.

The budget indicates that a saving of $235 million will be made in Medicaid by putting limits on federal reimbursement for the use of long-term care facilities. At the same time, legislation has been proposed to increase the federal government's share of payments for outpatient clinics, comprehensive health centers, and home services. The objective is to encourage the use of these less expensive facilities in preference to hospital care.

Funds for the National Center for Health Services Research and Development are increased somewhat, as are funds for medical manpower. The number of new places anticipated in medical schools, however, is modest. Indeed, some medical schools may find the net contribution of the federal government reduced as a result of a cut in funds for medical research and training.

Impact of the 1971 Budget

The 1971 budget decisions influence not only the level of public investment in health, education, and income support, but also the types of benefits provided and their allocation among different segments of the population.

Assistance to the Poor

Title I of ESEA, public assistance, Medicaid, and several other programs are aimed primarily at improving the position of the poor. But the federal government has other objectives as well. Medical research, library support, and college construction, for example, are general programs not directed at the poor alone.

How much emphasis should be placed on the needs of the poor relative to those of the population as a whole? The question is not just a matter of distribution. It is also a question of long-run strategy in helping the poor. It can be argued that in the end the poor may benefit more from a breakthrough in educational technology than from increases in present antipoverty services. The problem of priorities, however, becomes most acute in a tight budget year. The 1971 budget responds to these questions by channeling an increasing proportion of funds into programs aimed directly at the poor. (See Table 3-3.) The priority accorded to the poor derives partly from explicit decisions to fight poverty, most notably through the welfare reform. In addition, statutory entitlements enacted in previous years dictated uncontrollable increases in major programs for the poor.

Money versus Provision of Services

One persistent issue that pervades the HEW budget is whether to give individuals the means to purchase goods and services or to make public efforts to provide such goods and services. This budget moves substantially in the direction of payments to individuals.

In the mid-1960s, the nation rediscovered poverty and turned federal attention to improving the lives of the poor. The "war against poverty" emphasized breaking the cycle of poverty by reducing de-

Table 3-3. Budget Obligations for Major Programs for the Poor, Department of Health, Education, and Welfare, Fiscal Years 1969 and 1971

Millions of dollars

Program	1969 actual	1971 estimate
Public assistance and Medicaid	**6,231**	**8,989**
All other programs	**2,139**	**2,765**
Social services	717	1,046
Elementary and secondary education	1,134	1,325
Indian health	114	163
Educational opportunity grants	146	186
Other	28	45
Total	**8,370**	**11,754**
Total as a percentage of regular HEW budget	58	67

Source: *The Budget of the United States Government, Fiscal Year 1971—Appendix.*

pendency. New programs provided training, compensatory education, health care, and other services mainly designed to help the poor to become more productive. The strategy was an investment strategy, not an income maintenance strategy. Although public assistance and other income maintenance payments rose, no strong attempt was made to redesign the complex income transfer system or to move to a more general and adequate system of redistributing income to the poor.

The administration's budget presages a shift toward an income maintenance strategy. Although the proposed family assistance plan is budgeted at only $500 million in 1971, it represents a substantial reform in the welfare system with major future implications and costs. The apparent income maintenance strategy does not, however, preclude investments in the productivity of the poor. The Work Incentive Program (WIN) and vocational rehabilitation programs, for example, are given substantial increases. However, Title I of ESEA is not substantially increased, apparently because of doubts about the effectiveness of compensatory education as a weapon against poverty.

HEALTH FINANCING VERSUS PROVISION OF HEALTH SERVICES. A similar issue arises in health. Where the objective of the government is to increase the consumption of health services by certain groups, such as the poor and the aged, it can support institutions that provide those services (veterans' hospitals or neighborhood health centers, for example), or it can give consumers money for the purchase of health services. Although the budget provides some increases in funding for neighborhood health centers, the major emphasis continues to be on financing the consumption of health services; Medicaid and Medicare are rising fractions of the total HEW budget for health (Table 3-4).

Table 3-4. Budget Obligations for Health Programs, Department of Health, Education, and Welfare, Fiscal Years 1967, 1969, and 1971

Millions of dollars

Program	1967	1969	1971
Medicare	4,456	8,248	11,268
Medicaid	1,187	2,275	2,879
Other health programs	2,865	3,588	3,703
Total	8,508	14,111	17,850
Medicare and Medicaid obligations as a			
percentage of total	*66*	*75*	*79*

Source: *The Budget of the United States Government . . . Appendix,* for Fiscal Years 1969 and 1971.

STUDENT VERSUS INSTITUTIONAL AID. The government has a similar choice of providing aid to students or to the colleges and universities. Traditionally HEW has done both, but student aid had risen in importance in the previous administration. This budget suggests a continuation of the trend toward a student aid strategy—the higher education programs of the Office of Education will be almost exclusively student support programs (Table 3-5). The shift to student aid is even more pronounced than it appears in the table because of the concurrent shift from direct student loans to guaranteed bank loans,

Future versus Current Services

Funds for research and training in education and health are investments in the future provision of services. A breakthrough in health or education research, or in training new kinds of teachers or health personnel, could profoundly affect the provision of health and education services in the future. A basic issue, therefore, is how funds should be allocated between the relatively certain present and the relatively uncertain future.

In health, the provision of current services through Medicare and Medicaid dominates the picture. This is in contrast to the rapid

Table 3-5. Budget Obligations for Institutional and Student Aid in Higher Education, U.S. Office of Education, Fiscal Years 1967, 1969, and 1971

Millions of dollars

Program	1967	1969	1971
Institutional aid	583	337	108
Student aid	440	544	706
Total	1,023	880	813
Student aid as a percentage of total	*43*	*62*	*87*

Source: *The Budget of the United States Government ... Appendix*, for Fiscal Years 1969 and 1971. Figures are rounded and may not add to totals.

growth of medical research in the early 1960s and the relatively low priority accorded services at that time. This budget holds medical research funds virtually constant. More is provided for training medical personnel and less for research personnel. It is not clear whether the net effect of these various changes is an increase or a decrease in federal support for medical schools.

In education, by contrast, the emphasis has traditionally been on current services rather than research and training. The 1971 budget, perhaps because of rising doubts about the effectiveness of education methods, favors research and training. The expansion is from a small base, however. It should be remembered that biomedical research accounts for over $1 billion in the HEW budget, while HEW's funds for education research are barely a tenth that amount. (Education research financed in the Office of Economic Opportunity budget also is slated for a significant increase in 1971.)

Categorical versus General Aid

In both education and health, numerous special programs (often called categorical) were enacted in the 1950s and 1960s to support specific kinds of activity. There is fairly wide agreement that there are too many such programs and that their complex and sometimes conflicting guidelines make them difficult to administer and often unresponsive to local needs. A major question is the extent to which these categorical programs should be consolidated and replaced with more general and flexible forms of aid.

The administration inherited a policy of consolidating some categorical health programs—primarily those for the control of specific diseases—under Comprehensive Health Planning and Services. This strategy is continued in the present budget. It should be noted, however, that a new categorical program is also created: grants for family planning services.

In education there is currently no general aid program that can absorb the categorical aids. The administration's budget request primarily reallocates funds among the different categorical programs. An alternative strategy would have been to consolidate impacted aid, Title I, and the categorical programs into a new general aid program. This strategy probably would have required substantial budget increases to compensate the losers and would have encumbered federal efforts to specify the use of Title I funds by school districts.

Social Security

The thirty-five-year-old social security system is the basic system of income support for the elderly and disabled in this country. Payments of over $2 billion a month are now made to 25 million retired, disabled, and dependent persons; about 60 percent of these payments go to individuals and families who otherwise would be poor. The system has widespread public support and virtually no one questions the need for it.

The system has been modified and expanded many times since it was established in 1935, but its primary mission has remained the provision of income to the aged and disabled, financed through social insurance taxes. In September 1969, President Nixon proposed many changes in the structure and operations of the system as well as a 10 percent increase in benefit payments. In the closing days of the 1969 session, the Congress tacked a 15 percent benefit increase onto the Tax Reform Act and made a few small adjustments in the system, but took no action on most of the reforms recommended by the President.

Among the issues that are likely to be considered are the adequacy of the benefit structure, the maximum earnings limitation, methods of protecting benefits against the inroads of inflation, and the financing of the system.

The Benefit Structure

The 15 percent increase effective in January 1970 raised the average benefit for an aged couple from $170 to $196 a month, and minimum benefits from $55 to $64 for a single person and from $82.50 to $96 for a couple. There is widespread agreement that the minimum benefit is an expensive device to help the aged and disabled poor, because many who are eligible for the minimum benefit are also eligible for other retirement benefits.

An alternative to the increase in minimum benefits would be to extend the new family assistance plan to the needy aged, blind, and disabled. Although this approach would increase the cost of the family assistance plan, it would attack the problem of minimum benefits without diverting scarce budget funds to those who are already entitled to more than one retirement benefit. Those who are eligible for social security benefits that exceed the amounts provided by the family assistance plan would not be affected, while those with inadequate social security benefits would receive family assistance payments that would be reduced, and ultimately disappear, as the total income of the beneficiary increased.

This dual system would also be more flexible than the existing system. At present, any effort to improve minimum social security benefits to help the needy aged and disabled must in practice be joined with a general benefit increase. Under the dual system, the social security benefit could be set at any desired percentage of past earnings, while the family assistance plan would take up the slack for those who had not earned enough to be eligible for adequate social security benefits. The family assistance program proposed by the President has the advantage that it can be readily modified into such a dual, comprehensive system when budgetary conditions permit. Opposition to such a system would come from those who would object to the introduction of a "means test" into social security, but this objection could be overcome by keeping family assistance for the aged and disabled separate from social security.

The Earnings Limitation

From the beginning, social security has been a retirement system, not an annuity system. The distinction is often overlooked by those who believe that social security beneficiaries should be allowed to earn as much as they can. In a retirement system, the emphasis is placed on providing enough benefits to permit the retired worker and his family to live decently. Restrictions on payments to older persons with earnings reduce costs and thus permit the payment of larger benefits for those who do retire.

Under current law, a beneficiary may earn $1,680 a year ($140 a month) without loss of benefits; benefits are reduced $1 for each $2 of earnings between $1,680 and $2,880; beyond $2,880, benefits are reduced dollar for dollar. This limitation has been criticized on the ground that it reduces the work incentives of aged persons. On the other hand, it is recognized that its liberalization or removal would increase the incomes of those among the aged who are least in need.

The President has proposed a modification in the earnings limitation to correct for the rise in earnings that has occurred since the present provision became effective on January 1, 1968. Under his proposal, the limitation would be raised from $1,680 to $1,800 a year ($150 a month); for earnings above $1,800 benefits would be reduced $1 for each $2 of earnings. The President has also recommended that the earnings exemption be adjusted upward automatically in proportion to increases in future earnings levels. The currently proposed 7 percent increase is far below the rise in average earnings of production workers since January 1968, but this is balanced by the complete removal of the dollar-for-dollar reduction above the exemption.

An alternative to the earnings exemption is the "delayed retirement credit." Under this arrangement, beneficiaries who earn income would have their benefits reduced, but their future benefits would be increased by the full or partial actuarial value of the foregone benefits. This approach would increase work incentives at a relatively substantial—but deferred—cost to the system.

Adjustments for Inflation

Since the average life expectancy of a worker at retirement is almost fifteen years, inflation can seriously erode the real value of the benefits paid under the social security program. For example, if prices rose by only 2 percent a year, the real value of benefits would be reduced about 26 percent after fifteen years; if the rise in prices were 5 percent a year (the recent rate), the real annual value of the pension would be cut in half within fifteen years.

The argument against automatic adjustment of benefits for inflation is that, like other escalator clauses, it might tend to institutionalize inflation. If price increases were automatically translated into higher money incomes, any increase in the price level would tend to persist because money demand would continue to rise disproportionately and the price-wage spiral would be perpetuated. Nevertheless, failure to adjust social security benefits for price changes imposes a major share of the burden of fighting inflation on the groups that are least able to protect themselves against rising prices. When he proposed a 10 percent increase in benefits, the President also recommended that an automatic adjustment for price inflation be made every year. But the 15 percent increase adopted by the Congress is higher than the actual rate of inflation since 1968. Accordingly, it is unclear whether the President still wants an inflation adjustment to be made later this year. (The budget estimates are based on a continuation of the benefit schedules currently in effect.)

Suggestions have been made from time to time to increase the maximum earnings on which benefits (and taxes) are calculated to the point where the proportion of total wages covered would be approximately the same as that in 1939. This would mean an increase in the maximum to at least $15,000 under present circumstances. Such an increase would be justified if it were decided that society should be responsible for providing pensions for persons earning as much as $15,000 a year. There is no objective way of settling this issue, but the present $7,800 and proposed $9,000 are both in the neighborhood of median family *income* ($7,970 in 1967 and $8,630 in 1968), which is somewhat higher than median earnings. Thus, the $9,000 figure (and the future adjusted figures) would cover the earnings of workers who are roughly in the lower half of the earnings distribution.

Financing Social Security

Social security is financed by an earnings tax on workers, their employers, and the self-employed. These taxes are earmarked for insurance trust funds for old age and survivors (OASI), disability (DI), and hospital costs (HI). The estimates of the actuarial requirements of the OASI and DI funds are based on projections of earnings that assume no future increase in wage rates and benefit levels. Projections of the HI fund, on the other hand, assume that earnings levels and hospital costs will rise in the future. Since 1966, when the current inflation began, the balances of the OASI and DI funds have risen sharply because the very rapid increases in wages have more than offset the higher benefits that went into effect in February 1968. In contrast, the hospital insurance trust fund has been hard hit by the steep rise in hospital costs. The combined employer-employee payroll tax is scheduled under existing law to rise from 9.6 percent to

10.4 percent on January 1, 1971. The President has requested that 0.6 percent of this increase be shifted from the OASI and DI trust funds to the HI fund to avert a deficit in that fund.

At the benefit rates that went into effect in January 1970, the OASI and DI funds together will have a cash surplus of approximately $3 billion in 1971. The surplus will grow in future years as receipts rise in response to higher wage rates, scheduled increases in tax rates, and the President's proposed increase in the taxable wage base from $7,800 to $9,000.

These developments raise a number of issues. First, the large surpluses that have been accumulating in the OASDI trust funds have clearly been welcome from the standpoint of fiscal policy. The $1.3 billion estimated surplus in the budget for fiscal year 1971 would become a deficit of about $1.7 billion without the cash surplus in these trust funds. However, the justice of relying on payroll taxation for the budgetary margin needed to fight inflation is arguable, because the tax places a heavy burden on the poor. The criticism could be met if the payroll taxes paid by the poor were refunded to them. This would cost $800 million a year if only the employee tax is refunded, and $1.5 billion if both the employer and employee taxes are refunded. Refunds of both taxes would be justified if the tax is borne by the workers, as many economists believe.

Second, the OASDI surpluses projected for the year ahead are large enough to finance upward adjustments in benefits even beyond those needed merely to correct for the erosion due to inflation. However, the proposals made by the President in September 1969 adjust only for inflation. The maximum earnings on which benefits (and taxes) are calculated would also be adjusted upward in line with the rise in earnings levels. But these adjustments would still leave substantial surpluses in the OASDI funds.

In effect, the President proposes to use part of the OASDI surpluses for adjustments of OASDI benefits, part for another government program (health insurance), and the remainder for the budget surpluses that are needed for stabilization and other purposes. These decisions are debatable, but it is noteworthy that a President has made his recommendations in the context of the entire federal budget and his evaluation of the national priorities, rather than of the financial conditions of the trust funds alone.

4. Choices and Alternatives in Other Programs

THE DEPARTMENTS of Defense and Health, Education, and Welfare together account for 65 percent of the federal budget. Their programs and activities were considered in the two preceding chapters. The present chapter is concerned with priorities and program strategies reflected in the remainder of the budget. As before, the approach is selective rather than comprehensive. The subjects and the issues they raise were chosen to illustrate the difficulty and importance of decisions taken in the budget—not the dollar magnitudes of the programs involved.

Housing and Community Development

During the past thirty-five years, the federal government has launched a variety of programs to assist housing directly and to create favorable conditions for private housing construction. The budget does not fully reflect the cost and magnitude of these activities; many of them are not reported in the budget, and total housing expenditures are substantially offset by the sale of governmental assets. During 1971 federal outlays for direct housing assistance will continue to rise, largely as a result of commitments made in past years.

The government also undertakes Model Cities and urban renewal programs to advance the social and physical reconstruction of American cities. Expenditures under these programs in 1971 are expected to be $530 million and $1,035 million, respectively, compared to $300 million and $1,049 million in 1970.

The Housing Goal

In 1968 the Congress and the President set a goal for the national economy to build or rehabilitate 26.2 million housing units during the decade 1969–78. This goal reflected widespread concern that the sharp projected increase in net family formation from 34,000 in 1965 to more than 1 million in 1976,[1] increasing use of seasonal homes, an intensified effort to remove inadequate housing from the housing stock, and low vacancy rates would cause a severe housing shortage and huge increases in rents and home prices. As part of this goal the federal government pledged to subsidize the housing costs of low- and moderate-income families and thereby support the building or rehabilitation of 6 million units. Private (unassisted) housing starts were projected at 20.2 million over the decade. These figures excluded the production of mobile homes.

In the Second Annual Report on National Housing Goals, President Nixon revised the goal by including mobile homes within the definition of housing units. The administration forecasts that 4 million mobile homes will be built during the goal decade. Since most mobile homes are thought to be principal residences, their inclusion broadens and improves the definition of housing units, but it also implies a reduction of 4 million units in the goal as originally defined. The composition of assisted construction also has been altered; the number of units to be newly constructed has been increased, while the number of rehabilitations has been reduced by 1 million. Moreover, the sum of assisted starts and rehabilitations is now projected to be smaller each year through fiscal year 1971 and larger thereafter than was projected in 1969. (See Table 4-1.)

Residential construction starts and rehabilitations in fiscal year 1969 totaled 1,638,000 units and shipments of mobile homes totaled 363,000, far below the annual average of 2,600,000 units necessary to meet the goal. In large measure this shortfall was anticipated. Monetary conditions and previous levels of construction activity led Presi-

Table 4-1. Comparison of 1969 and 1970 Projections of Housing Starts, Rehabilitations, and Mobile Homes, Various Fiscal Years, 1969–78

Thousands of housing units

Housing and federal involvement	1969	1970	1971	1975	1978	1969–78 total[a]
New housing starts						
1969 projection, total	1,625	1,900	2,075	2,700	2,975	24,200
1970 projection, total	1,597[b]	1,350	1,505	2,550	2,545	21,000
Federally unassisted						
1969 projection	1,450	1,500	1,600	2,300	2,600	20,200
1970 projection	1,440[b]	1,090	1,060	1,955	1,960	16,000
Federally assisted						
1969 projection	175	400	475	400	375	4,000
1970 projection	157[b]	260	445	595	585	5,000
Rehabilitations, federally assisted						
1969 projection	50	100	150	250	325	2,000
1970 projection	41[b]	50	60	135	137	1,000
Mobile homes, federally unassisted						
1969 projection	n.i.	n.i.	n.i.	n.i.	n.i.	n.i.
1970 projection	363	450	475	400	312	4,000
Total starts and rehabilitations						
1969 projection	1,675	2,000	2,225	2,950	3,300	26,200
1970 projection	2,001[b]	1,850	2,040	3,085	2,994	26,000

Sources: *First Annual Report on National Housing Goals*, Message from the President of the United States, H. Doc. 91–63, 91 Cong. 1 sess. (1969), p. 17, and data to be published in the forthcoming *Second Annual Report on National Housing Goals.*
n.i. = not included.
a. Includes intervening years not shown in the table.
b. Reflects actual starts and rehabilitations for fiscal 1969.

dent Johnson to forecast in January 1969 that 1,675,000 units would be started and rehabilitated, of which 225,000 would be publicly assisted. In fact about this number were started, although publicly assisted units were somewhat fewer and the unassisted ones somewhat more than the original projection.

The housing issues for the 1970s are how to bring about the massive increase in residential construction needed to achieve the housing goal and whether the American people are prepared to take the necessary steps and incur the associated costs. To reach the goal would require that the fraction of gross national product devoted to residential construction rise from 3.5 percent to more than 4 percent a year. A substantial budget surplus at full employment of perhaps $10 billion a year might well be necessary to assure an adequate flow of savings to finance residential construction and other forms of investment. Since an excess of federal revenues over expenditures withdraws purchasing power from the income stream, a budget surplus provides a form of national saving. With a surplus, monetary policy can be easier than would otherwise be possible; credit can be made more freely available, and interest rates can be lower. In turn, housing construction tends to respond more readily to changes in credit conditions than do other sectors of the economy. Using the surplus to repay some of the federal debt can support this strategy by freeing investment funds tied up in government securities, at least some of which will be reinvested in mortgages. As an alternative, the government could use the surplus to buy mortgages directly or to pump funds into institutions that buy mortgages. From an accounting standpoint, this would reduce the surplus because such purchases of mortgages are treated as budget outlays. But from an economic standpoint, the government would be using its "surplus" to channel funds directly into housing finance, rather than to depend on the indirect effects of debt retirement.

Federally Assisted Housing

Three indicators may be used to measure the volume of federal assistance; unfortunately, each may tell a different story. The process of building or rehabilitating a unit begins with a *reservation* or similar indication of federal willingness to support further work. A reservation is a federal promise to provide some form of assistance to builders, local housing authorities, owners, or tenants. After an interval varying from less than a year to three or four years, depending on the program, construction or rehabilitation begins. For new units this step is recorded as a *housing start.* After the unit is completed, federal assistance begins and *expenditures* occur. In some cases, reservations may apply to existing units so that the second step is skipped. Because expenditures cannot occur unless there has first been a reservation and usually a start (or rehabilitation), and because several years may pass between reservations and expenditures, one indicator of program activity may be rising while another is falling.

In addition, most federal assistance takes the form of a long-term commitment to make annual payments of various kinds. Thus expenditures not only begin long after reservations, but also extend far into the future. Even if all reservations were to cease and federally assisted housing starts then dropped to zero, housing assistance expenditures would continue to grow for a few years and would not end until roughly one decade into the twenty-first century. To put it another way, a constant number of reservations and assisted housing starts implies a steadily increasing level of expenditures under federal programs of housing assistance. Reservations are probably the best indicator of *current* program activity, while expenditures are a measure of the *total* activity, past and present.

The federal government directly assists residential construction and rehabilitation through a large number of programs administered by the Department of Housing and Urban Development and the Farmers Home Administration (FmHA). The methods of providing housing subsidies vary, but in all programs the federal government reduces the net cost of new housing, or of improvements in old housing, to existing or prospective tenants. A brief description of the six major forms of assistance follows:

Low-rent public housing. Local housing authorities buy, build, or lease units for which the federal government pays all capital costs and some operating costs for financially hard-pressed authorities, to assure that no tenant must pay more than 25 percent of family income in rent. In recent years an increasing proportion of new public housing has been built for the aged, predominantly white. Median income of tenants in public housing in 1967 was $2,800, virtually unchanged in real terms for more than a decade. In 1969 federal contributions averaged $1,057 annually per unit of new public housing.

Rent supplements. Eligible low-income households pay one-fourth of their income in rent in certain buildings owned by nonprofit or limited dividend bodies while the federal government pays the difference up to 70 percent of a fair market rent. As tenant incomes rise, their rents rise until they reach market rentals, but unlike public housing occupants, these tenants are not required to leave, however high their incomes climb. Median income of tenants in rent supplement units in 1969 was $2,400 and the cost to the government for each unit was $1,128.

Section 236 rental assistance. Tenants pay 25 percent of income in rents up to an income level at which rentals equal fair market rents. Project owners negotiate mortgages at commercial interest rates. The government pays owners the difference between rents paid and costs incurred by the owner. The government payment is limited to the difference between actual mortgage payments and those that would be payable had the loan been made at 1 percent. In practice the maximum subsidy is slightly more

than one-third of market rents. This limitation means that tenants bene-
fiting from section 236 assistance must have considerably higher incomes
than those of rent supplement tenants. In 1969, federal contributions
averaged $804 per unit.

Section 235 homeownership assistance. This program is similar to section
236 except that assistance goes to owner occupants, who are required to
spend 20 percent of income on mortgage payments. As with section 236,
the same limitation on federal assistance means that very low-income
households will not be eligible. Average income of section 235 homeowners
was reported in 1969 to be $5,346, and federal contributions averaged
$756 per unit.

Section *221(d)(3) rental assistance.* Under this program nonprofit or
limited dividend owners could obtain 3 percent mortgages on approved
projects. Banks were willing to make below market interest rate (BMIR)
loans only because the Government National Mortgage Association
bought them at par. This program is being replaced by section 236 rental
assistance because the 221(d) (3) subsidy was undifferentiated with respect
to tenant income and because of budgetary considerations described
below. The annual equivalent subsidy per unit in 1969 was estimated at
$349.

Farmers Home Administration (FmHA) insured loans. These loans are
made at below-market rates predominantly to low- and moderate-income
rural households. FmHA then sells them at market rates to private investors, making up the difference between market and face value over the
life of the loan out of appropriations. All loans are in rural areas or in
towns of 5,500 or less. Median income of borrowers in fiscal 1969 was
$6,000. One distinguishing aspect of FmHA loans is the great hesitance of
FmHA to foreclose on borrowers. The average loan in 1969 was $9,866.

With some minor exceptions, the level of *reservations* planned for
1971 is already of the magnitude required by the goal for subsidized
housing. (See Table 4-2.) In the publicly assisted programs as a whole,
starts and *completions* will rise sharply in future years. (See Table 4-3.)
Section 236 (rental subsidies) and section 235 (homeownership assistance) are relatively new programs, so that even though reservations
will not increase after 1971, starts and completions will rise markedly
in response to those high reservation levels. These programs resemble
a long assembly line from which finished products begin to emerge
only after a time. Low rent public housing presents a somewhat different picture. It is an older program and reservations have been substantial for some years; consequently the future increase in starts will not
be as dramatic.

Expenditures for public housing, rent supplements, and sections

235 and 236 depend not on reservations, starts, or completions in any one year, but on the total number of units completed in all previous years. For example, the federal government supports low rent public housing by paying local housing authorities enough to cover amorti-

Table 4-2. Level of Federal Housing Applications, Reservations, and Loans, Selected Programs, Fiscal Years 1969–71

Program	Indicator	*1969 actual*	*1970 in 1970 budget estimate*	*1970 in 1971 budget estimate*	*1971 estimate*
			Number of units		
Low rent public housing	Applications approved	195,004	140,000	100,000	110,000
Rent supplement	Reservations	18,905	96,700	46,700	68,100
Homeownership assistance (Sec. 235)	Reservations	27,698	143,000	145,700	148,500
Rental assistance (Sec. 236)	Reservations	21,637	143,900	133,100	141,700
Farmers Home Administration rural housing loans	Loans	44,397	136,840	79,500	143,500
Total		307,641	660,440	505,000	611,800

Source: *The Budget of the United States Government . . . Appendix*, for Fiscal Years 1970 and 1971; U.S. Department of Housing and Urban Development; U.S. Bureau of the Budget.

Table 4-3. Targets for Federally Assisted Housing Programs, Various Fiscal Years, 1969–75

Program	*1969 actual*	*1970 estimate*	*1971 estimate*	*1975 projected*
	Thousands of units started or rehabilitated			
Low rent public housing	79	102	100	145
Rent supplement[a]	17	22	14	35
Below market interest rate (Sec. 221(d)(3))	44	28	11	0
Homeownership assistance (Sec. 235)	3	48	145	175
Rental assistance (Sec. 236)	1	17	77	175
Farmers Home Administration home loans	33	63	121	172
Other	21	28	35	28
Total	199	308	503	730

Source: From data to be published in *Second Annual Report on National Housing Goals*. Details may not add to totals because of rounding.
a. Includes only units started or rehabilitated under Sec. 221 market rate program.

zation on forty-year bonds sold by the local housing authority to private investors. When a public housing project is completed, there begins a forty-year federal obligation to cover the annual amortization. Thus, federal expenditures for public housing will rise as long as the number of public housing units increases. (See Table 4-4.) Even if the 1971 budget prohibited construction of any new public housing beyond units already approved, a substantial number of units would become eligible for subsidy in 1971 and 1972. As a result, increases in budget outlays for low rent public housing in 1971 are not really subject to control by the administration, and those in 1972 are controllable only to a very limited extent. Decisions on public housing expressed in the 1971 budget will have their primary effect in 1973 and later. A similar situation exists with respect to rent supplements and sections 235 and 236. The fact that section 221(d)(3)(BMIR) calls for the full cost to be paid when the project is completed, rather than for yearly amortization or interest subsidies over the life of the project, partly explains why this program is being replaced.

The situation with respect to loans insured by the Farmers Home Administration (FmHA) is different in detail but not in principle. The 1971 budget calls for $1.4 billion in such loans to 143,500 borrowers, an increase from $784 million in loans to 79,500 borrowers in 1970. However, the budget calls for $1.7 billion more in net asset sales by FmHA in 1971 than in 1970. Proceeds from such sales are used to offset new direct outlays and have the effect of reducing budget outlay

Table 4-4. Expenditures or Obligations for Federally Assisted Housing Programs, Fiscal Years 1970, 1971, and 1975

Millions of dollars

	Expenditures or obligations		
Program	1970 estimate	1971 projection	1975 projection
Low rent public housing (*expenditures*)	453	644	1,304
Rent supplement (*obligations*)	22	47	312
Homeownership assistance (Sec. 235) (*obligations*)	19	84	595
Rental assistance (Sec. 236) (*obligations*)	2	21	424
Special assistance function of Government National Mortgage Association (*expenditures*)ᵃ	546	617	n.e.
Total	1,042	1,413	2,635

Source: *The Budget of the United States Government, Fiscal Year 1971—Appendix*, and authors' estimates.
n.e. = not estimated.
a. Expenditures are primarily for the purchase of below market interest rate mortgages made under Sec. 221(d)(3) of the National Housing Act, which is being replaced by Sec. 236 housing.

totals. In fact, as a result of these sales, net outlays under this program for fiscal 1971 appear in the budget as *minus* $636.1 million, which in turn serves to reduce total budget expenditures by this amount.

The housing goal implies the need to assure the construction and rehabilitation of 600,000 subsidized units a year, and reservations planned for 1971 will approach that level. But different housing programs reach different economic groups. Public housing and rent supplements reach families at or below the poverty line, while programs such as FmHA loans reach households with somewhat higher incomes. The geographic impact of housing policies also differs among programs. Thus FmHA loans reach only rural areas and small towns; from 55 to 61 percent of its borrowers in recent years have lived in the southeastern quadrant of the United States. Activity under other programs is spread more evenly throughout the country and among large cities and small towns. For example, 8 percent of all public housing units on December 31, 1967, were in towns of less than 5,000 population and 33 percent were in the South.

Federal assistance may be used to encourage either homeownership or renting. Rent supplements, low-rent public housing, and section 236 rental assistance all encourage construction of rental units. Section 235 homeownership assistance and FmHA loans go predominantly to homeowners. Federal assistance can also be used to encourage either rehabilitation of existing units or construction of new units, though federal policy traditionally has favored new units. Several programs have focused on home improvements and repairs, and on major rehabilitations, but the emphasis has been on the first of these. As a result, very few seriously deteriorated units have been rehabilitated.

The one major program increase in the housing area in the 1971 budget—the expansion of loans insured and subsidized by the Farmers Home Administration—suggests somewhat more attention to moderate-income homeowners in small southeastern towns and on farms, and relatively less to low-income households in larger cities and in the West, East, and North.

Private Housing

Perhaps the key element of federal policy affecting the construction of private housing is the government's monetary and fiscal posture. Conditions in the money market strongly affect the flow of credit to home mortgages. In the context of efforts to moderate inflation, the greater the fiscal restraint in the budget, the less the need for restrictive monetary policies. In a related vein, the less the federal government must borrow, the more private savings are available for investment in home mortgages. The 1971 budget probably projects a small surplus rather than a deficit in part because the administration concluded that the more stringent monetary policies required by a deficit budget would have left the housing industry virtually starved for mortgage credit.

The substantial increases in effective housing demand projected for 1973 and later years pose a continuing budgetary problem. It seems likely that under normal full employment conditions, private businesses and households will not save enough to finance the needs of business expansion and the housing goals as well. To attain the housing goals without curtailing private investment, the government may have to run substantial budget surpluses.

In addition to monetary and fiscal policy, several specific federal programs affect the construction of private housing. The Federal Housing Administration (FHA) and the Veterans Administration (VA) protect lenders against default by borrowers. The 1971 budget projects an increase from 329,000 to 424,000 in the number of units committed to be built or rehabilitated under mortgage insurance and loan guarantees. It also anticipates an increase from 742,000 to 846,000 in the number of existing units on which FHA mortgage insurance or VA loan guarantees are given. These projected increases reflect the expectation expressed in the President's Economic Report and the budget that monetary conditions will ease, resulting in increased demand for housing.

Neither FHA nor VA will generate net budgetary expenditures in 1971. FHA mortgage insurance is supported by fees levied on borrowers; in recent years the fees have more than covered net costs of the insurance. In the event of a serious economic slowdown, this situation could be reversed. VA loan guarantees are supported by direct appropriations, but net expenditures for these guarantees are scheduled to drop by $336 million as a result of sales of assets.

Two quasi-public institutions help to stabilize the flow of mortgage credit. Since both are privately owned, their operations are excluded from the budget. In fiscal 1971 the Federal Home Loan Bank Board (FHLBB) is expected to advance some $2.4 billion to more than 4,500 savings and loan associations from the proceeds from sales of its own bonds, a decline from $4.5 billion in fiscal 1970. The Federal National Mortgage Association (FNMA) creates a secondary market for government-insured and -guaranteed mortgages by buying (and at times selling) such mortgages with the proceeds from sales of its own bonds. In fiscal 1971 FNMA is expected to buy $4.8 billion in home mortgages, down from $5.7 billion in fiscal 1970. These operations will give rise to budget outlays in neither fiscal year 1970 nor 1971. Not all FHLBB advances or FNMA purchases represent a net increase in funds available for mortgages, since some of the funds that investors are expected to spend on FHLBB and FNMA bonds would otherwise have found their way to the mortgage market.

The Government National Mortgage Association (GNMA) is a recently created agency within the Department of Housing and Urban Development. Of its several functions, the most important for this discussion is the assistance it provides to the financing of subsidized housing. In many instances private investors are unwilling to make FHA-insured loans under sections 235 and 236 and other programs at rates allowed by FHA. GNMA steps in and buys the mortgages at face value; it then marks down the prices to the market level and sells them to the privately owned FNMA. Thus the federal government is able to assist in financing subsidized housing without incurring large immediate budget costs.

Building Costs and "Operation Breakthrough"

Gross hourly earnings rose nearly twice as fast in construction as in manufacturing in 1969, in part because of union restrictions on the training of additional construction workers. In addition, some building codes and work rules limit the introduction of new cost-saving devices and materials. Interest costs, which form a larger part of the cost of housing than of most other goods, have risen sharply in recent years. As a result of these factors, housing costs have risen much faster than the costs of most other commodities. Finally, a great many housing units—especially those constructed by small firms—are built by old-style handcraft methods not amenable to the factory or mass production techniques that have increased productivity in other industries.

To overcome these handicaps, the government has undertaken Operation Breakthrough, which, according to the 1971 budget, is "designed to demonstrate the economic feasibility of high-volume housing production techniques and remove market constraints that inhibit their use." Largely as a result of Operation Breakthrough, $55 million is requested for urban technology and research, compared with $11 million in 1969.

The outcome of Operation Breakthrough is important but uncertain. A large drop in construction costs would enable the country to attain the housing goal at much less expense and thus increase the possibility of fulfillment. Reductions in the costs of new housing would also affect the price of existing units for which new units are substitutes. Major cost reductions will be very difficult to achieve, however. Some large-scale builders use mass production methods, but not to the extent employed in several other countries. Transportation costs on finished units or modules will continue to be high, and substantial on-site work—such as building the foundation—will continue to be necessary. Costly work rules and restrictive building codes are difficult to change. Moreover, two major components of housing costs—land and interest—are subject to independent influence. All these conditions and constraints suggest that some cost reductions can be achieved through improvements in housing technology, but not to the extent hoped for by many governmental and housing officials. Over time, the payoff from Operation Breakthrough may depend on increasing the supply of construction labor sufficiently to hold construction wages in line with those of other industries.

Community Development: Model Cities

In its present form, the Model Cities program is essentially a system of block grants to cities, conditioned on the submission of satisfactory local plans for helping disadvantaged areas. The plans are to provide for a concerted effort to improve education, skill training, employment, health, welfare, and physical development using federal, state, local, and private resources. As with other grants or with revenue sharing, the principal issues are the amounts to be granted or shared, the governmental organs designated to receive the transfers, and the kinds of restrictions to be imposed.

The program works in two stages. First, cities apply for "planning grants." If the applications are approved, they receive funds to carry out studies to identify urban problems and develop programs for their solution. On completion of a satisfactory plan, the cities become eligible for "supplementary grants," which constitute the heart of the Model Cities program. These grants are used to cover up to 80 percent of the nonfederal costs of carrying out the approved plan. Nonfederal costs include (1) expenditures that otherwise would be borne wholly by state or local governments or by private organizations, and (2) the state or local shares under grant programs partially supported by the federal government through other appropriations. Each dollar in supplementary grants is expected to be combined with several dollars of total expenditures from federal and other sources. The size of these contributions is crucial to the success of Model Cities.

By fiscal 1969, 150 cities had been made eligible for planning grants. It was expected that all of them would be receiving supplementary grants, many for only part of a year, during fiscal 1970. It now appears that all 150 may not begin to receive supplementary grants until fiscal 1971.

Although still young, the program has undergone several shifts in emphasis. The Johnson administration originally envisaged massive expenditures in five to ten cities to demonstrate that great improvements in the urban environment were feasible. Because of political obstacles, plans to concentrate spending on a handful of cities in order to produce spectacular results were discarded in favor of the current approach of providing more modest help to a substantial, but still limited, number of cities. The first cities were required to focus their planning and funds on neighborhoods holding the most urgent problems and not more than 10 percent (or 15,000) of the city's population. Moreover, the Department of Housing and Urban Development required that cities accord considerable voice in planning to community organizations within affected neighborhoods. The present administration has removed the requirement that a Model Cities plan focus on particular neighborhoods, so that entire cities may be included. In addition it has determined that neighborhood organizations—particularly those created to participate in Model Cities—are to have relatively less voice in planning than was previously intended. It is these changes that have converted the Model Cities program into something approaching a block grant for cities.

The 1971 budget contemplates a slowdown in growth and perhaps a major cutback in the eventual scale of Model Cities. The Johnson administration requested $750 million for the program in fiscal 1970 and anticipated that grants of about $1 billion a year would be distributed among 150 cities when all began to receive supplementary grants for full years. Further increases would follow as the cities increased their ability to use the funds effectively. The new administration reduced the fiscal year 1970 request to $675 million because it estimated that cities would be ready for supplementary grants later than had been anticipated when the budget was drawn up. The Congress approved $575 million.

In preparing the 1971 budget the administration faced a choice of two broad alternatives. On the one hand, Model Cities could be steadily expanded through increased grants to currently eligible cities, through an increase in the number of eligible cities, or through a combination of these measures. On the other, the program could be held at roughly the present levels or cut back and other forms of assistance to cities or states be expanded as funds became available. The budget request for 1971 is $575 million—the same as actual appropriations for the preceding year. However, because cities have been even slower to become eligible for supplementary grants than the administration expected in mid-1969, a large backlog of unused budget authority will permit $670 million to be obligated during fiscal 1971. Nonetheless it seems clear that the administration has decided to keep the Model Cities program smaller than originally intended, at least until pressures on the budget have declined. There is no indication that more cities will be added to the list of those eligible for supplementary grants.

Urban Renewal

The urban renewal program, begun in 1949, is the oldest and largest federal program for improving the physical condition of cities and towns. Some 2,531 urban renewal plans are expected to be approved by the end of 1971, nearly two-fifths of them since 1965. But the completion of urban renewal programs takes many years, sometimes more than a decade. Only 733 programs are expected to be completed by the end of 1971, and only $5.2 billion of $10 billion in cumulative authorizations will have been spent. (See Table 4-5.) In any year the volume of urban renewal activity under way from previous years is far greater than the volume of new programs undertaken or of old programs completed.

Table 4-5. Cumulative Grant Reservations and Disbursements for Urban Renewal, Various Fiscal Years, 1955–71

Millions of dollars

Fiscal year	Approved grants	
	Reserved	Disbursed
1955	445.4	52.9
1960	1,644.1	311.2
1965	4,539.0	1,294.5
1969	8,037.5	3,114.9
1970 (estimate)	9,037.5	4,163.9
1971 (estimate)	10,037.5	5,198.9

Sources: *Independent Offices and Department of Housing and Urban Development Appropriations for 1970*, Hearings before a House Subcommittee of the Committee on Appropriations, 91 Cong. 1 sess. (1969), Pt. 4, pp. 152–53; *The Budget of the United States Government, Fiscal Year 1971—Appendix.*

For many years most urban renewal projects followed a common pattern. A geographical area was designated a renewal area. Initial commitments from the federal government were obtained. A local public agency (LPA), through purchase or eminent domain, acquired all real property within the renewal area and razed existing structures. The LPA then sold the cleared land to private developers or allocated it for public buildings, often obtaining additional federal commitments. The federal government contributed financially to these operations by paying moving allowances to displaced families and by paying up to two-thirds of the difference between the LPA's total expenditure and its receipts from the sale of cleared land.

Critics of the program objected to the severe disruption of existing neighborhood patterns and the slowness of execution. As a result the Congress has liberalized allowances for displaced families. Increasing effort is being made to prevent the replacement of poor but cheap housing, occupied mostly by blacks, with good but costly housing that mainly whites can afford, or with office buildings. Continuing concern that urban renewal was drastically reducing the supply of low-cost housing led the Congress in 1969 to stipulate that cities must build as many new low- and moderate-cost housing units as are demolished during renewal.

Many neighborhoods can be improved through selective rather than total renewal, at less cost in money and with less disruption. Accordingly, in 1968 the Congress authorized local agencies to submit plans annually for spot demolition, spot construction, and spot code enforcement, and to receive funds to cover one year's work rather than the whole project. The Congress and the administration hoped that this approach would reduce the proportion of total budget authority tied up in grants not likely to be spent for many years. This new approach, called the Neighborhood Development Program (NDP), was so popular that requests from cities for NDPs mushroomed during fiscal 1970. Because NDP grants are usually spent much faster than other urban renewal grants, the administration in April 1969 limited to thirty-five the number of cities eligible for NDP. The 1970 budget had anticipated that the number would grow to seventy-five in June 1969 and 150 in June 1970, but only thirty more NDPs had been approved and announced by February 11, 1970. Although the budget does not state the proportion of urban renewal capital grants to be allocated to NDPs during 1971, Secretary Romney has said that the amount will be about $350 million.

Both the Johnson and Nixon administrations requested $1 billion for the total urban renewal program for fiscal 1970, and the Congress appropriated that amount. Last year the Nixon administration withdrew a Johnson request for advanced appropriation of $1.25 billion for fiscal 1971; it has now requested $1 billion for that year, the same as actual contract authority approved for fiscal 1970. The leveling off in budget requests and the freezing of NDP mean that urban renewal outlays, which lag behind contracts, will stop growing in 1971. In addition the administration appears to be less willing than was usual in the past to approve supplemental requests for ongoing renewal projects. If rigorously pursued, this policy will make funds available for new projects. (See Table 4-6.)

Secretary Romney testified in June 1969 before a subcommittee of the Senate Appropriations Committee that the administration would

Table 4-6. Grant Authority and Outlays for Urban Renewal, Various Fiscal Years, 1955–71

Thousands of dollars

Fiscal year	Authority	Outlays
1955	0	33,500
1960	350,000	104,300
1965	750,000	282,528
1969	1,062,500	533,793
1970	1,000,000	1,049,000
1971 (requested)	1,000,000	1,035,000

Source: Same as Table 4-5.

submit a proposal in 1970 to merge Model Cities and urban renewal into a single program. Such a merger would require many changes in the way cities formulate urban renewal plans and in the character of Model Cities.

Manpower

During the 1960s, federally supported manpower programs became an integral part of economic and social policy. Most of these activities are administered by the Department of Labor, the Department of Health, Education, and Welfare, and the Office of Economic Opportunity. They focus on the job needs of the unemployed, the poorly educated, and the unskilled. Anticipated outlays for these programs during fiscal 1971 will amount to $2.8 billion, a fifteenfold rise in the past decade and an increase of 18 percent from the preceeding year. (See Table 4-7.)

The Assistance Now Available

Manpower programs in the federal government have grown piecemeal over the years and seek to serve many different purposes.

The Public Employment Service was created in 1933 to administer the unemployment insurance program and to help place in jobs those

**Table 4-7. Federal Outlays for Manpower Programs,
Various Fiscal Years, 1961–71[a]**

Millions of dollars

	Outlays				
Type of program	1961	1964	1967	1970	1971
Institutional training	—	93	566	658	739
On-the-job training	—	5	53	280	469
Work experience and work support	—	—	388	425	458
Job placement and support	126	181	306	390	454
Administration, research, and support	4	17	92	132	157
Vocational rehabilitation	54	84	215	500	553
Total	184	380	1,619	2,385	2,830

Source: Compilation by Sar A. Levitan based on information from the U.S. Bureau of the Budget. Details may not add to totals because of rounding.
a. Includes only outlays by the Departments of Labor and Health, Education, and Welfare.

who were drawing unemployment insurance. Until recently its efforts were primarily concentrated on the experienced unemployed—those who had held a steady job but who were put out of work by economic circumstances.

Since the 1920s the federal government has supported the training and rehabilitation of the physically handicapped through the Vocational Rehabilitation Program, as substantially modified and broadened by the Vocational Rehabilitation Acts of 1965 and 1968.

Broad-scale manpower training programs for those other than the physically disabled were authorized by the Manpower Development and Training Act (MDTA) of 1962. Special programs of work and training for relief recipients also date back to 1962, but the current Work Incentive Program (WIN) was authorized by the 1967 amendments to the Social Security Act. The family assistance plan proposed by the present administration would expand still further various manpower programs for relief recipients. The Economic Opportunity Act of 1964 and subsequent amendments created several other specialized programs providing work, training, or other manpower services for the hard-core unemployed. The Job Corps, Neighborhood Youth Corps, and Public Service Careers are the major examples.

Using authorities and funds provided by many legislative acts, several packages of manpower services have been created by administrative action, including particularly Job Opportunities in the Business Sector (JOBS) and the Concentrated Employment Program (CEP). Five basic kinds of manpower services are available through these various programs:

1. Skill training, adult education, and other remedial measures imparted in an institutional setting rather than on the job. The Job Corps and parts of MDT and WIN are devoted to such institutional training.

2. On-the-job training (OJT), in which adult education, skill training, and remedial measures are carried on at job sites. The JOBS program is the major example.

3. Job creation and work experience. Programs in this category provide work (Neighborhood Youth Corps) and in some cases seek to develop new types of jobs for the hard-core unemployed, for example as paramedical personnel and education aides (Public Service Careers).

4. Job placement, counseling, recruitment for training programs, and related manpower services. The Public Employment Service handles most of these programs, although the Concentrated Employ-

ment Program, WIN, and Vocational Rehabilitation often purchase such services for their clients from other public or private agencies.

5. Rehabilitation of the physically handicapped. The Vocational Rehabilitation Program was broadened in 1965 to include persons whose handicap is due to social, educational, or other disadvantages.

Recent Changes in Programs and Policies

The Manpower Development and Training Act of 1962 for the first time created large-scale federal training programs for the unemployed. In their early days, these programs continued the emphasis on the experienced unemployed, who were often high-school graduates needing new skills because their former jobs had been eliminated. With the adoption of the poverty program in 1964, however, increasing emphasis began to be placed on providing services to the hard-core unemployed. A large proportion of these persons have not had a high-school education and have not previously held a skilled or semi-skilled job. They tend to be young people—particularly teenage and young adult blacks in the inner city—and mothers of broken families trying to support their children. Increasingly the federal manpower programs have also come to incorporate more than technical training and to include remedial education and services designed to inculcate desirable work habits.

"Hire First, Train Later"

Following the policy advocated in the last year of the Johnson administration, the manpower programs in fiscal 1969 and 1970 have emphasized job placement more than training on the assumption that the latter will come with job experience. They have relied on private employers rather than public institutions not only to create the jobs but also to provide the training. Initially, MDT focused on institutional training because on-the-job training opportunities were scarce in the early 1960s, when unemployment exceeded 5 percent. As the labor market tightened in 1965, OJT became more appealing because it required less government outlay per trainee than did institutional training (training allowances were unnecessary since employers paid wages to trainees) and because of the linkage between training and jobs with private employers. Followup statistics indicated that more than nine of every ten OJT enrollees were employed one year after completing the course of training, compared with two of every three institutional trainees. Because employers were to be reimbursed for the direct cost of OJT, they were encouraged to hire workers who might otherwise have remained unemployed.

But the subsidies paid to private employers under MDT-OJT covered only the cost of instruction and materials, and employers creamed off the best-qualified applicants. To induce employers to hire, train, and retain the hard-core unemployed, the government declared that it was ready to raise the ante, and the JOBS program was established in January 1968. Businessmen pledged to hire the disadvantaged unemployed and to provide not only jobs and training but also a full range of supportive services needed to encourage the new employees to retain their jobs.

The National Alliance of Businessmen (NAB), organized to coordinate private sector participation in the JOBS program, has claimed that since the program's inception in January 1968, some 269,000 disadvantaged jobless persons had been hired and that 143,000 were still on the job in November 1969. Employers sought reimbursement, however, for only about one-fourth of all reported placements. In December 1969, only 35,000 workers were employed under JOBS contracts with the Department of Labor.

It is difficult to explain the reluctance of employers to accept reimbursement offered under JOBS, although some observers believe that even the minimal government involvement in JOBS is more than many businessmen will accept. Reflecting the Labor Department's anticipated difficulty in spending the $420 million allocated to the program by the Johnson and Nixon administrations for fiscal 1970, the amount available for new obligations was reduced to $300 million in fiscal 1970 and raised to only $375 million for 1971. Government subsidies under JOBS ranged from $200 to $6,000 per man-year and averaged close to $3,000, or about double the amount paid under MDT-OJT.

Reducing the Job Corps Program

The most striking change during the first year of the Nixon administration was the sharp curtailment of the Job Corps. Many impartial observers of manpower programs questioned whether Job Corps results, as evidenced by low retention rates and little educational advancement, justified the high average annual costs of nearly $8,000 per enrollee. The administration revamped the program by shifting it from the Office of Economic Opportunity to the Department of Labor, closing fifty-nine (presumably the least effective) of 123 centers, and replacing them by February 1970 with only four non-residential centers. There is little question that the Job Corps needed reform, though it has been argued that the cuts were too rapid and that alternative opportunities for Job Corps clients were often not provided.

Major Issues in the 1971 Budget

The administration's budget and legislative requests raise several important questions about the future of these programs.

Management Improvement

A number of separate legislative and executive actions have resulted in a series of categorical manpower programs administered by three different federal agencies and numerous local sponsoring organizations under diverse regulations controlling eligibility, allowances, and types of services offered. Appropriations are made separately to a host of different programs, and transfers from one program to another to meet local needs are impossible. As a consequence, even when funds are available for labor market services, few clients receive the precise package they need, and participants usually qualify to receive only selected kinds of aid.

The administration has proposed a new manpower training act to consolidate many of these diverse programs. The act would make it possible to use appropriated funds flexibly for a wide variety of manpower services, in contrast to the current separation of funds into watertight compartments. It would also rely on the states as primary administrators of the program, while charging the secretary of labor with responsibility for monitoring federally funded programs to ensure that federal objectives are being met. Although the program would be basically turned over to the states, the secretary of labor would retain 20 to 25 percent of the total manpower funds for research, evaluation, experimentation, and demonstration, as well as for initiation of projects where states and localities do not carry out federal objectives.

Under the act, the secretary of labor would gradually turn over responsibility to each state as it demonstrated the capacity to organize, plan, and deliver manpower services in accordance with broad national objectives. Experience with other programs, however, has demonstrated that once basic control passes to the state or local government, it is almost impossible for the federal government to exercise a significant voice in how the funds are spent. Efforts to maintain federal standards by authorizing federal agencies to approve state plans often do not work, since those agencies are most reluctant to resort to cutting off program funds. Consequently the critical problem for the Congress and the administration is to design a series of realistic and very specific criteria—in statutory language and in administrative regulations—that must be met by state governments at each step in the process of turning the federal manpower programs over to them. Unless such criteria are developed and unless they are clear and precise, the secretary of labor will find it a very difficult political feat, even in the best of circumstances, to ensure that state government manpower organizations, programs, and policies have reached the level at which a transfer of powers and responsibilities would be warranted.

Employing Relief Recipients

The current public assistance program, through amendments adopted in 1967, puts great emphasis on training relief recipients and helping them secure jobs. The Work Incentive Program (WIN) is devoted to this purpose. The administration's new welfare program, the family assistance plan, proposes to continue this emphasis on finding work for welfare recipients, and $600 million of the first full-year cost of the family assistance plan is to be devoted to training and other work programs, through an expansion of WIN and related activities. This reflects the clear desire of the Congress and the administration to shift welfare beneficiaries from relief rolls to payrolls as a means of halting and reversing the rapid growth in welfare costs. Several major obstacles stand in the way of this objective, however.

In the past the public assistance programs have provided little incentive for recipients to find and keep a job. Until recently, for every dollar earned on a job, an equivalent amount was deducted from the relief check. In 1967 the program was modified to allow welfare recipients to keep the first $30 of monthly earnings and one-third of any additional amount—hardly a powerful work incentive. The new family assistance plan substantially strengthens work incentives; welfare recipients may keep the first $60 a month of outside earnings plus half of any additional amount. These incentive features should remove, or at least substantially weaken, one of the major obstacles to the employment of welfare recipients. On the other hand, as noted in the earlier discussion of the family assistance plan, work incentives are diminished by the fact that the value of food stamps and other subsidies is reduced when earnings increase.

The degree to which the welfare rolls can be reduced by placing welfare recipients in jobs depends upon how many of them are potentially employable. It is commonly believed that the great majority of welfare recipients can, through training and job placement programs, be placed in steady employment. An HEW analysis of the characteristics of welfare recipients indicates that this is, at best, a costly process, applicable only to certain welfare recipients. (See Table 4-8.) It is estimated that 3.9 million family heads will be eligible for assistance under the family assistance plan. Of that total, 1.3 million are already working full time and another 500,000 are aged, ill, or disabled. The remaining 2.1 million able-bodied people who are working part time or not at all are presumably the major target of training and placement programs. But of this 2.1 million, some 122,000 are already

Table 4-8. Families Eligible for Family Assistance Program, by Employment Characteristic, Projections for Fiscal Year 1971

Employment characteristic		Thousands of family heads
Working full time		1,271
Aged, ill, or disabled		488
Working part time or not at all:		
Working part time all year	122	
Working full time most of year	529	
Mothers with dependents needing supervision[a]	790	
All others	657	
Subtotal		2,098[b]
Total number of potential recipients		3,857

Source: U.S. Department of Health, Education, and Welfare; and authors' computations.

a. This category includes 575,000 mothers with children under six and 215,000 female family heads who, in response to a survey, indicated they were not working because they were caring for home or family. Some family heads in this category do work intermittently, but not enough to be classified in either of the preceding categories.

b. This subtotal comprises 931,000 males and 1,167,000 females.

working at year-round part-time jobs. Another 529,000 work full time most of the year and presumably are out of work for part of the year because of plant layoffs, local economic slack, or similar reasons. While job placement and training programs might be useful in some cases, economic circumstances probably determine their job experience. Hence the primary target is the 1.4 million people who work only intermittently or not at all. This group constitutes about 40 percent of those eligible for assistance—a large but not overwhelming proportion.

Of the 1.4 million "primary targets," some 575,000 are women with children under age six, and another 215,000 have other dependents needing care. If public policy requires that these women be trained for useful jobs and be employed full time, then day-care centers will have to be established for their children. Experience with Head Start and other preschool programs shows that adequate day care, with careful supervision and educational content, may cost $1,000 to $1,500 a year for each child. Part-time supervisory arrangements for younger school-age children involve somewhat lower costs. The average welfare family has three children under age eighteen. If we assume that the total number of children under six who will need day care is 700,000 and that another 500,000 older children will need some form of supervision, annual budget expenditures on day care of more than $1 billion will be needed. And this does not take into account the possibility that many mothers now working full time at low-paying jobs will place their children in day-care centers.

To train welfare recipients for jobs paying wages high enough to remove them in large part, if not entirely, from the welfare rolls will not be an easy task. Some 560,000 of the potential trainees live in rural areas where the population is so scattered that the provision of manpower services is difficult. Almost 900,000 have a grade-school education or less, and a large part of the remainder did not finish high school. Thus, remedial education, as well as skill training, will be necessary.

Rise in Unemployment

While the shift in recent years from institutional to on-the-job training has undoubtedly increased the effectiveness of manpower programs, it has also made them much more sensitive to fluctuations in the labor market. Employers would find it difficult to hire or retain disadvantaged workers when they were laying off employees with greater seniority; resistance to the training and placement of relief recipients would increase, since they would be competing for scarce jobs with workers recently unemployed. Whatever the achievement of JOBS thus far, a slack labor market would sharply reduce its potential. This would probably result not only in the reallocation of JOBS funds to institutional training or in the subsidization of public employment, but also in the aggregate expansion of outlays for manpower programs.

The administration's manpower training act proposes an automatic trigger mechanism to raise appropriations for selected manpower programs by 10 percent if unemployment rises to 4.5 percent for three consecutive months. At the present level of appropriations, this would boost the funds allocated to manpower programs at an annual rate of about $170 million. The proposed additional funds are adequate to provide for only a small minority of the prospective victims of involuntary idleness. According to Labor Department estimates, a rise of unemployment from 3.4 percent (the level at the end of 1969) to 4.5 percent would, during the course of one year, raise the number of persons unemployed fifteen weeks or longer from 2.5 million to 3.9 million; the number of persons unemployed more than twenty-six weeks during the year would rise from 1 million to 1.8 million. More than $2 billion would be required—again using Labor Department estimates—to absorb the increase in the long-term unemployed under MDT or work experience programs. But when unemployment is high and jobs are scarce, trainees who would benefit from the $2 billion would face a bleak prospect at the end of their training period.

To meet these dilemmas, several courses of action might be considered, some of which have already been suggested by the administration. First, unemployment insurance could be liberalized to provide more income to the experienced unemployed. The administration has proposed that the unemployment insurance laws be amended to provide an automatic extension of unemployment insurance when the rate of insured unemployment reaches 4.5 percent (about equivalent to a 5.7 percent total unemployment rate). This percentage trigger could, of course, be set at various alternative levels. Second, with more flexible manpower programs, emphasis could be shifted from training to temporary public employment as a holding action for some of the unemployed until the labor market tightens up and more jobs become available to trainees. Third, to provide appropriations of the magnitude needed to handle the problem, the trigger mechanism for manpower appropriations might provide for a new increment of appropriations each time the unemployment rate rises by a certain amount, rather than simply calling for a single 10 percent increase when the rate rises above 4.5 percent.

Transportation

In 1971 the federal government will spend some $8 billion on transportation programs. Almost 60 percent of the total will be spent on highway programs, including safety and beautification; 20 percent will be devoted to various forms of aid to civil aviation; and 17 percent will be spent on water transportation, both domestic and ocean going. (See Table 4-9.)

Table 4-9. Budget Outlays for Transportation, by Mode, Fiscal Year 1971

Mode of transportation	Millions of dollars	Percent of total
Highways	4,588	58
Aviation	1,678	21
Water	1,330	17
Other programs	348	4
Total[a]	7,944	100

Sources: *The Budget of the United States Government, Fiscal Year 1971; Special Analyses, Budget of the United States, Fiscal Year 1971.*
a. Calculated before deducting proprietary receipts of $121 million.

This pattern of investment in transportation is strongly affected by history and precedent. The federal government has long assumed almost sole responsibility for financing investments in inland waterways and in air traffic control and navigation facilities. Since the Merchant Marine Act of 1936 it has financed a large share of private construction of ocean going ships. And since the Federal-Aid Highway Act of 1956, it has carried most of the burden of financing superhighway construction. Today the operating and investment outlays for these three modes of transportation account for more than nine-tenths of the federal transportation budget. The trend in federal outlays since 1955 is shown in Table 4-10.

Table 4-10. Budget Outlays for Transportation, by Agency, Various Fiscal Years, 1955–71

Millions of dollars

Agency and type of transportation	1955	1960	1965	1970	1971
Department of Transportation:					
Highway	636	2,978	4,069	4,642	4,588
Aviation	122	508	756	1,252	1,636
Railroad	2	3	3	21	23
Coast Guard	190	238	367	593	597
Urban mass transit	0	0	11	158	280
Other programs	0	0	23	33	46
Proprietary receipts (−)	0	0	−20	−26	−121
Subtotal	950	3,727	5,209	6,673	7,049
Other agencies:					
Army Corps of Engineers (navigation projects)	118	202	396	385	400
Civil Aeronautics Board	61	67	92	48	42
Maritime Administration	163	270	330	318	333
Subtotal	342	539	818	751	775
Total	1,292	4,266	6,027	7,424	7,824

Sources: For 1955, 1960, and 1965, James R. Nelson, "Future Federal Transportation Budgets: Basic Numbers and Anticipated Budget Issues" (unpublished paper, 1969); for 1970, 1971, see sources for Table 4-9.

In this century, almost all investment in railroad facilities has been private. In the case of urban mass transit, most investment has been made until recently either by municipal governments (subway systems) or by private firms (commuter trains and many bus systems). Federally aided urban highways provide routes for urban bus systems, but the great bulk of federal highway aid has been devoted to interstate highways rather than urban streets. In recent years a modest amount of federal aid for investment in urban mass transit systems has been forthcoming, and the new budget proposes to expand that assistance.

Transportation programs are financed in part by the general taxpayer and in part by specific taxes, or user charges, levied on those who use the facilities. The proportion of federal transportation outlays that is covered by user charges varies widely from program to program. Highway users, through taxes on gasoline, oil, tires, and trucks, pay for highway aid. Commercial airline users, primarily through a tax on passenger tickets, pay for much but not all of their use of federal aviation aids. Owners of private planes, on the other hand, pay only a minuscule fraction of the cost that their use of the airways imposes on the federal government. Most of this investment is paid for by the general taxpayer. Similarly the general taxpayer, not the waterway user, pays for federal investment and maintenance costs on inland waterways. The general taxpayer also foots the bill for the cost of maritime subsidies and assistance to urban mass transit.

The 1971 budget proposes new expenditure programs or user charges in four areas: highways, aviation, urban mass transit, and the merchant marine. This section examines existing and proposed programs in the first three. The merchant marine subsidy program is discussed in the next chapter, which reviews a number of long-standing federal programs.

Aviation

Two distinct types of civil aviation are recognized—*commercial airlines* carrying passengers and freight, and *general aviation*, which consists of private planes flown for business or pleasure. Both have grown and continue to grow very rapidly. In the past decade the number of commercial passenger air miles flown has risen at an average rate of 13 percent a year. The growth of general aviation has been even more pronounced. As against 69,000 private planes in 1959, in 1969 an estimated 131,000 private aircraft were flying the airways, compared to 2,000 commercial airliners.

Of the many ways the federal government supports this growth, three are particularly important. First, the government builds and operates the navigation and traffic control facilities for en route aircraft. It also constructs and operates the terminal traffic control and landing aid facilities at airports. Finally, it provides grants-in-aid to state and municipal governments for constructing and improving airports. Total outlays of the Federal Aviation Administration (FAA) for building and operating facilities and for airport grants are estimated to be $1.3 billion in fiscal 1971.

The rapid growth of aviation and stringent safety standards have put great pressure on the federal budget. Excluding the cost of developing the supersonic transport, expenditures of the FAA have almost doubled since 1964. Even so, the expansion of facilities has not kept pace with the growth in demand. Together with a growing scarcity of airspace around major airports, the shortfall has led to increasing congestion and delay. These problems stem in part from the very fact that aviation facilities are provided at cut rates or even free to important segments of the industry. Charges levied on commercial aviation currently cover about 70 percent of the costs incurred by FAA in providing facilities and services to commercial airlines. Charges on general aviation (levied as a small tax on gasoline) pay about 5 percent of the costs attributable to general aviation activity.

Like any good that is underpriced, traffic control and other facilities tend to be overused. Because the general taxpayer covers a large part of the bill, flying—particularly flying a private plane for business or pleasure—is much less expensive to the flier than the true cost of the activity. Appropriate user charges can therefore serve two purposes: to place the cost of providing facilities on those who use them rather than on the general taxpayer, and to discourage excessive use of scarce facilities and airspace, thereby relieving congestion. ("Excessive" in this case refers to the use of airway and terminal facilities by persons who would not use them if they had to pay the full cost.)

For a number of years, successive administrations have sought to impose user charges high enough to cover the costs of these facilities. Principally because of opposition from representatives of general aviation, the proposals have never been enacted. The last budget of the Johnson administration proposed a new strategy that has been adopted in the 1971 budget transmitted by the Nixon administration. It seeks no substantial increase in appropriations for FAA's facilities and operating budget or for its grants-in-aid to airports, despite the growing demand for FAA's services. However, the administration has indicated that once its recommendations for increased user charges are adopted, it will request a $293 million supplemental appropriation for additional facilities, operations, and airport grants. In short, it is following a pay-as-you-go approach, which in effect tells the industry: "If you will agree to pay for the added services, we in turn will make the necessary financing available."

The proposed user charges, in the aggregate, would pay most of FAA's costs by 1975. Even so, two important questions could be raised.

First, should higher charges be levied on general aviation? Even with the new charges, general aviation would be paying only about one-quarter of the costs allocable to its activities. From the standpoint both of equity and of discouraging excessive use and congestion of airspace, higher charges on general aviation may be warranted.

Second, should user charges be restructured to reflect more accurately the composition of FAA's costs? Almost all of the proposed charges are closely related to the number of passenger miles flown in the case of commercial aviation, and to aircraft miles flown in the case of general aviation. They include taxes of 8 percent on commercial airline passengers, 5 percent on air freight waybills, 9 cents a gallon on fuel used in general aviation, and a $3 departure tax on international passengers. But FAA's costs are sensitive not only to the number of miles flown between airports, but also to the number and spacing of landings and takeoffs at airports. Between now and 1975, almost half of FAA's costs for new facilities and equipment will be attributable to the construction and operation of facilities at air terminals. User charges related to landings and takeoffs—for example, landing and takeoff fees—would have several advantages: (1) They would tend to discourage excessive use at crowded major airports, where the greatest delay and congestion occur; (2) the fees could be varied according to the time of day to encourage use during congestion-free periods and to discourage use during peak hours; (3) they would provide FAA with better measures of the actual economic demand for terminal facilities and thus lead to more efficient investment decisions.

The real costs of congestion at airports far exceed the costs to FAA. Congestion wastes valuable passenger time and imposes large additional direct operating costs on the airlines (from circling in a holding pattern, burning fuel while waiting to take off, and so on). For example, during a two-hour period of congestion involving 100 commercial aircraft at a major airport, only ten general aviation flights spaced evenly over the two hours would cause a delay of 500 aircraft minutes. Conservatively assuming sixty passengers on each commercial flight, those ten general aviation flights—serving perhaps twenty or thirty passengers—would result in an aggregate delay of 30,000 passenger minutes (500 passenger hours) and additional direct operating costs to the commercial carriers of about $5,000. If passenger time is valued conservatively at $3 an hour, each general aviation flight under those conditions costs, in terms of delay, $500 in direct operating outlays and $150 in passenger time.

It might be asked whether increased congestion causes accidents. Since it is almost always possible to provide for safety by rigid rationing of airspace, safety can be bought at the cost of delays. Hence the shortage of FAA facilities need not itself lead to lower safety, though it does lead to greater delay. Only if a decision were made to relax safety standards in the interests of reducing delays would safety necessarily deteriorate. Therefore the real question is whether user charges can be enacted in types and amounts that will provide the financing and the incentives needed to reduce delays.

Highways

Although the federal government has long provided financial assistance to state and local governments for highway construction, very large federal outlays for this purpose did not begin until the Federal-Aid Highway Act was approved in 1956. The government then undertook to pay 90 percent of the right-of-way and construction costs of a 42,500-mile interstate highway system and to continue paying 50 percent of the costs of primary and secondary roads. Special taxes on gasoline, oil, tires, and trucks are channeled into a highway trust fund from which these expenditures are made. The interstate system was scheduled to be completed by 1972, but administrative limits on trust fund expenditures, rising costs, and the growing difficulty of securing land and local agreement to construct the urban segments of the system have delayed completion, which may not occur until 1974 or 1975.

Until 1966, highway expenditures closely matched trust fund revenues each year. In fact the rate at which trust fund revenues were collected was the main limitation on spending. Between 1956 and 1966, federally aided highway expenditures rose from $740 million a year to $4 billion a year. Since 1967, however, highway grants-in-aid have been held below revenues each year as a means of reducing inflationary pressure. Thus revenues and expenditures approximately balanced each other at $4 billion in 1966, but federally aided expenditures will have grown to only $4.4 billion by 1971 while tax revenues will amount to approximately $5.5 billion. As a consequence the trust fund will have built up a surplus of unexpended revenues of some $3.4 billion by the end of 1971. Therefore, barring a continued hold-down in expenditures, the potential exists for a large increase in highway expenditures in the years immediately ahead.

Two major sets of policy choices are currently at issue in the highway program. One of them pertains to the 1971 budget, the other to the longer-term budgetary outlook.

Studies of factors contributing to highway costs have shown that, compared with automobiles and light trucks, large trucks appear to be paying less than their full share of the burden. To remedy this situation the administration is requesting increases in the tax on diesel fuel and in the use taxes on heavy trucks. These measures would add $260 million to revenues in 1971 and somewhat larger amounts in subsequent years. However, presumably because of the desire to increase total government revenues, the proposed increase in taxes on trucks is not balanced by suggested reductions in other highway taxes. Consequently the total revenues of the highway trust fund will be increased at a time when revenues are already running substantially above expenditures and there is a large surplus in the fund. So long as the basic trust fund concept is retained, these additional revenues will increase the pressure for higher outlays in future years.

As the surplus continues to grow, and in the light of requests for additional highway taxes, the question of retaining the trust fund concept arises. Whether highway expenditures should grow in the near future to $6 billion or $6.5 billion (to match revenues and reduce the accumulated surplus) might properly be considered a matter of national priorities rather than an issue to be decided mechanically on the basis of trust fund revenues. If the priority approach is to govern decisions on future highway expenditures, perhaps the trust fund approach should be abandoned formally, as it has been abandoned in practice in recent years.

Turning to the longer-term problem, the administration will soon have to submit to the Congress its proposals for a successor to the existing highway program. As noted earlier, the interstate system will be almost complete by 1974, but highway taxes, if extended, will be yielding some $6 billion a year in revenues. Because of the long lead time for preparing, debating, and undertaking a major transportation program, proposals for subsequent federal aid to highways and the future of highway taxes will have to come soon. Some major issues will then confront the administration and the Congress.

1. Should a new highway program be devised along the lines of the present one? In particular, should a tabulation of highway needs based on traffic projections by state highway departments serve as the basis for the new program as it has served for the existing one? There are two dangers in this approach. First, as massive new freeways are completed, their very existence creates new traffic. Rather than demand calling forth a supply of highway investment, the investment creates its own demand. Second, highway needs cannot be determined

except in conjunction with knowledge of competing modes of transportation. Depending on federal investment in the other modes, there may or may not be a need for a particular highway investment.

2. Should highways be considered as a separate program with its own federally determined allocation of funds, or should the federal program be so structured as to encourage states and localities to examine alternative uses of federal transportation assistance? One possible restructuring of federal transportation programs would establish an *urban* transportation program under which local officials could receive assistance for urban freeways, mass transit, or congestion-reducing projects, according to their needs, and an *intercity* transportation program that would encompass aid to highways, aviation, and high speed rail transit. Once the interstate system is completed, highway emphasis must shift from the creation of a basic national network to alleviation of spot problems of highway capacity, safety, and appearance. Broadening the conception of federal transportation programs along these lines would also require a rethinking of the current structure of user charges and general subsidies.

3. Should the trust fund concept be retained? A transportation program narrowly concerned with highways, or more broadly covering other forms of transportation, could be developed with or without the trust fund approach. The earmarking of revenue for a particular program should be judged on its own merits.

However these issues are decided, the administration and the Congress over the next year or two will have an opportunity to make fundamental decisions about the nature of the system. They need not be bound by the past history and existing structure of federal transportation programs.

Urban Mass Transit

In 1964 the Congress enacted a program whereby the federal government pays two-thirds of the net project cost of new or improved subways, commuter rail services, bus services, and the like. Net project cost is the part of the investment that cannot be repaid from passenger revenues. Thus the federal government in effect offers to pay two-thirds, while state and local governments must contribute one-third of the subsidy needed to bring the capital costs of new or improved systems into line with their revenue-generating potential.

Since the inception of this program, appropriations for mass transit capital grants have remained rather small; in fiscal 1970 they amounted to $175 million. Considering the heavy investment costs of major transit systems and the large number of eligible cities, this is not a large sum. The 1971 budget proposes a substantial expansion of these capital subsidies, and several features of the request are particularly important.

1. The program envisages $10 billion in assistance extending over twelve years. It would grow from $300 million in 1971 to $1 billion a year by 1975 and continue at that level through 1982:

Fiscal year	Proposed program level (millions of dollars)
1971	300
1972	400
1973	600
1974	800
1975–82	1,000

2. Building new mass transit systems or making major improvements in existing ones requires long preparation, a time-consuming effort to gain community approval, and a sizable investment in planning and engineering. Quite naturally, local governments and planning bodies are reluctant to spend the necessary time and money when the critical federal contribution depends on the year-to-year vagaries of the budget and appropriation processes. Consequently the administration considered following the example of the highway program by establishing an urban mass transit trust fund into which earmarked revenues would be channeled exclusively for the mass transit program. After much debate, this alternative was rejected on the grounds that a trust fund and earmarked revenues would tie the federal government's hands and make the annual level of federal support for mass transit subject not to considerations of priority and need, but to the annual yield of the trust fund.

3. A different alternative was adopted to meet the legitimate need of local planners for assurance that the federal budget will make funds available when they are required. The 1971 budget requests mass transit appropriations not just for 1971, but for the entire 1971–75 period; the Congress will be asked to approve $3.1 billion for the first five years of the program. Thus the program managers can begin making long-term plans with local governments for use of the funds over the next five years, though the actual commitment of

federal moneys will occur gradually. (Technically, the Congress is being asked to approve $3.1 billion in "contract authority," which will allow the administration to make binding commitments with local governments. As the commitments come due, the Congress must still appropriate funds to make good on the obligations, but this tends to be a formality since firm contractual commitments will already have been made.)

Issues and Alternatives

Several aspects of the proposed $10 billion in subsidies warrant particular attention, given the choices confronting the Congress and the administration. Federal subsidies to urban mass transit—which make possible a level of fares lower than full costs—can have three potential objectives: (1) to provide better transportation to inner-city residents and thereby broaden their employment opportunities; (2) to induce automobile commuters to switch to mass transit, thus relieving congestion on city streets; and (3) to provide speedier and more convenient transportation for suburban commuters who live relatively close to mass transit stations.

Of the $10 billion requested for the mass transit program, some $5.5 billion is tentatively destined for large new systems and $2.5 billion for improvements in existing large systems. Thus 80 percent of the funds will be devoted to large-scale mass transit projects, principally subways and commuter railroads. Some $1.5 billion will be used for small and medium-sized systems (principally bus services), and $500 million for research and development.

Since the large urban systems are already in the planning or construction stage, it is possible to suggest the patterns of transportation that will emerge, and how they relate to the three objectives noted above. The new systems will not be similar to the old, long-established subway systems of New York and Boston.[2] In general the new funds will help to build rapid rail transit facilities linking high-income suburbs and airports with downtown centers, as in San Francisco's Bay Area Rapid Transit (BART) and the Hopkins Airport extension in Cleveland; or they will buy new cars and other equipment for commuter railroads. Stations in the new systems will be separated by long distances compared with those in existing subways. The number of inner-city stops will be much smaller and the number beyond city limits much greater than in older systems. (BART, for example, will have eight of its seventy-five miles and twelve of its thirty-seven stations within the city limits; the existing Boston system, on the other hand, is concentrated within the central city and has almost fifty of its approximately seventy stations located within the city limits.) A significant part of the federal funds for urban mass transit will also go to commuter rail services. In other words, the new and improved systems will predominantly serve the suburban commuter with high speed and infrequent stops, and will concentrate relatively little on movement within the central city.

By their very characteristics—emphasis on high speed, few inner-city stations, and radial patterns—the new systems will do relatively little to open employment opportunities for the poor. Access to inner-city stations will be limited, and suburban stations will tend to serve outlying residential areas rather than industrial sites. But because the distances between stops on the new systems will be relatively long, the number of commuters who will switch from automobiles to mass transit will be limited by the problem of making the trip from home to suburban stations. Moreover, recent studies have indicated that as some commuters switch from automobiles to mass transit, thus relieving congestion, others who were carpooling switch to driving alone and thus vitiate much of the temporary ease in congestion. Indeed, alternatives to the automobile usually do not serve to reduce congestion. Rather, in the absence of heavy penalties on the use of downtown streets (for example, very high parking taxes), the inevitable increase in traffic seems to halt only when it is discouraged by congestion. In short, the ability of the new systems to relieve congestion on downtown streets and approaches should not be overestimated.

The basic value of the new systems will be to provide faster and more convenient transportation for a segment of the urban commuter population. That this is a limited objective does not imply that it is unworthy, though it does suggest two further considerations. (1) The new mass transit program should not be expected either to reduce downtown congestion significantly or to solve the transportation-related job problems of the low-income inner-city resident. (2) As the program develops, it may be worth reexamining the current emphasis on high-speed rail and subway systems to determine whether it should be somewhat lessened in favor of subsidized improvements in cross-town and inner-city transit services.

To the extent that improvement of urban mass transit systems is not effective in reducing congestion, specific penalties or disincentives on the use of heavily traveled streets may be the only alternative. Sophisticated electronic devices to levy tolls on the use of congested streets represent one avenue of approach. Modest support of research and development in this area might produce substantial future rewards. In the interim, downtown congestion might be limited by stringent parking regulations and stiff taxes on private parking spaces. While such matters are primarily in the hands of local authorities, the federal government could, through the planning requirements of its highway and urban mass transit programs, encourage them to consider such solutions.

As was suggested with respect to highways, the problem of urban transportation should be considered as a whole. Urban freeways, urban streets, extra bus lanes, off-street parking, subways, and commuter rail systems are all to some extent competitive with one another. How city planners choose a balance among them should depend upon how each contributes to safe, fast, and convenient transportation, with a minimum of disruption to neighborhoods and local amenities. The proper combination will vary from city to city according to geography, existing economic patterns, and planned future patterns. A rigid separation of federal aid into "highway" and "urban mass transit" categories, with different appropriations, authority, and grant criteria—and with statutory formulas governing the distribution of highway funds—could ultimately reduce the effectiveness of the assistance.

Pollution Control

Control of environmental pollution has become *the* issue of the day. Conservatives and liberals seek to surpass each other in denouncing the evils of pollution and in calling for its elimination. The Congress last year increased the funds for water pollution control grants from the $214 million that the President requested in the budget to $800 million, and the President agreed to spend the added funds even in the face of concern over a rising budget total. Almost every major newspaper and periodical has featured a series of reports on pollution. Students protesting involvement in the Vietnam war have transferred some of their concern to the pollution problem. Not surprisingly, the President's State of the Union Message, Economic Report, and budget this year gave great attention to the pollution issue, and in February a special presidential message on the quality of the environment was transmitted to the Congress.

In the short space available, only a few of the issues involved in the problem of environmental quality can be discussed. The emphasis here is on those specifically associated with existing and proposed federal programs to deal with air and water pollution. Several introductory comments are in order.

The Problem

The quality of the air and the quality of water are natural resources just like any other. Air and water assimilate the wastes that an industrial civilization produces. As the society grows, the quality of the air and water changes for the worse as the volume of wastes to be assimilated increases. Until recently we have treated those resources as free goods and have used them lavishly. In turn, the prices of industrial products have been lower because they did not include the costs of reducing or changing the waste products generated. As a consequence, our standards of living improved in one direction—relatively cheap and mass-produced products—while deteriorating in another—an increasingly polluted and unpleasant environment. To achieve the benefits of a better environment, this country will necessarily have to pay the costs, which essentially means that industrial output and community services will become more expensive as they give up the "free" use of the environment. Electric power output, for example, is expected to double by 1980. Cheap electric power is a keystone of high industrial productivity and convenient living. If it is produced with thermal plants, however, it pollutes the air. If it is produced with atomic power, it heats the water of our streams. Reducing the pollution consequences of producing electric power will inevitably add to the price of electricity, and the less the pollution content, the greater the increase in price.

These hard facts lead to three considerations: (1) The current concern over environmental quality is more likely to lead to lasting accomplishment if the costs as well as the benefits of pollution control are made clear. (2) An absolutely "pure" environment—with every river a mountain brook, every city blessed with desert-fresh air, and every species of animal protected against any possible ecological damage—is unachievable, except at a cost so monumental as to destroy most other aspects of our high living standards. As in other areas of human life, we must weigh benefits against costs and select that level of environmental quality that most nearly balances what we gain with what we lose. To view every use of pesticide or every emission of pollution as an absolute evil is neither realistic nor helpful to improvement of environmental quality. (3) Because the costs of reducing pollution are so high, the efficiency as well as the effectiveness of pollution control programs must be given attention. The more efficient the program, the more pollution control we buy for each dollar spent.

Federal Water Pollution Control Programs

Historically the federal government has developed two lines of attack on the problems of water pollution control. It makes grants to communities to build municipal waste treatment and handling facilities on the basis of priorities established by the states; $1.3 billion has been appropriated for this program since its inception in 1957. As noted above, $214 million was appropriated for the program in 1969, and in 1970, when the President requested the same amount, the Congress responded by appropriating $800 million.

The federal government also establishes water quality standards on interstate waters and through a complex and time-consuming enforcement procedure, attempts to control pollution, particularly by industry. Primarily this is a "uniform treatment and standards" approach to the problem and has not been notably successful. A number of its shortcomings were dramatically illustrated in a recent evaluation of the program by the General Accounting Office (GAO).

Problems in Current Programs

Until this year, a lack of funds held the grant program to the $200 million level, substantially below the amount needed to make significant progress towards meeting national water quality standards. In a 1969 report the Federal Water Pollution Control Agency (FWPCA) estimated the need for annual expenditures of about $1.7 billion for municipal treatment works and $1.3 billion for sewer construction. Compared with this $3 billion need, state and local expenditures for these purposes have been running at about $1 billion to $1.2 billion a year.

Pollution control also suffers from a lack of river basin planning. Efficient reduction of pollution in a river basin calls for a wide variety of integrated measures, including not only waste treatment plants but also regulation of stream flow, aeration, high-level chemical treatment

Table 4-11. Budget Obligations and Expenditures for Water and Air Pollution Control Programs, Fiscal Years 1965, 1970, and 1971

Millions of dollars

Program	1965	1970	1971
Water pollution control:			
Research	15	51	45
Construction grants	93	515	1,000
Other	19	47	54
Total obligations	127	613	1,099
Expenditures	*101*	*255*	*421*
Air pollution control:			
Research	n.a.	51	62
Abatement and limitation	n.a.	35	40
Other	n.a.	8	8
Total obligations	21	94	111
Expenditures	*16*	*80*	*104*

Source: *The Budget of the United States Government . . . Appendix*, for Fiscal Years 1967 and 1971. Figures are rounded and may not add to totals.
n.a. = not available.

during certain periods, and other basin-wide approaches. Moreover, once the river basin is considered as a system, it becomes clear that some waste treatment facilities will make a greater contribution than others to cleaning up a river basin, depending on where the facilities are located, the degree of current pollution, and the assimilative capacity of the river. In other words some facilities will yield greater effectiveness per dollar than others. But federal grants have usually been allocated to individual communities in accordance with priorities drawn up by each state, which have not ordinarily taken account of the cost-effectiveness of the facility. As a consequence, far less progress has been made than might have been the case.

In addition, current practice introduces formidable political difficulties. FWPCA and the states have aimed at uniform secondary treatment of municipal wastes in all communities. But faster progress could be made by evolving river basin plans that require speedier and more comprehensive action in some places along the river basin than in others, thereby maximizing the effectiveness of the dollars available. States find it politically difficult, however, to develop plans calling for differential treatment of wastes by different communities. Precisely those upstream communities that gain least from pollution control would bear the most expense, while the downstream communities that receive the most benefits would pay the least. Only a basin-wide system of charges on all communities will avoid disproportionate costs for some and windfalls for others, thereby laying the base for systematic planning and the assignment of cost-effective priorities.

In the absence of federal standards for construction of treatment plants, compounded by inadequate municipal provision of operating funds, a large number of plants have run at far less than full efficiency. In addition the federal grant program has tended to assist primarily the construction of new treatment plants and interceptor sewers. As a natural consequence, the completion of these facilities has come nearest to meeting national goals, while expansion and replacement of existing systems and construction of sanitary connecting sewers has lagged.

In a study of eight river basins, the GAO found that in recent years growing industrial pollution has overwhelmed the reduction in pollutants made possible by the construction of municipal waste treatment plants, usually with federal grants. Several shortcomings of pollution control policy have led to this result. Federal standards have applied only to interstate waters, and enforcement of water quality standards has been a very complex and time-consuming procedure. In addition, reducing industrial pollution by enforcing water quality standards through the judicial approach has some inherent weaknesses that simple streamlining of procedures and toughening of penalities may not overcome.

Pollution arises in large part because industry is not charged with the costs its wastes impose on society—it uses the river free. As a consequence, aside from the pressure of public opinion, industry has no incentive to minimize the cost of pollution, while it has every incentive to minimize the costs of other things it has to pay for—labor, steel, machinery, and so forth. Enforcing specific effluent standards on industry through court action is one approach to reducing industrial pollution. But it suffers from the disadvantages of an all-or-nothing technique; a finding must be made that a firm is or is not in violation of the law.

There may be need for an alternative approach that provides economic incentives to a firm to reduce pollution without requiring a case-by-case verdict of guilt. The levying of an "effluent charge" on industry, as practiced in parts of Europe, represents one such approach. Firms pay a tax on the amount of pollutants they discharge into the water. The less the pollution, the lower the tax bill. The tax rates can be set high enough to establish a powerful incentive for firms to adopt internal production methods that generate fewer pollutants, or, where that is uneconomic, to treat waste discharges to remove pollutants from them. This incentive to reduce pollution works primarily through the market rather than through judicial proceedings, and the combination of the market and the effluent tax schedule takes the place of fines and judgments.

The Administration's Proposals and the Issues They Raise

The President's budget and environmental message to the Congress propose a number of modifications in the current federal pollution control program.

INCREASED FUNDS. The President proposes a five-year, $10 billion program for waste treatment facilities. The federal government would provide $4 billion in grants; state and local governments would put up $6 billion. Federal grants would be committed at the rate of $1 billion a year for the next four years, and the program would be reevaluated at the end of that time. To assist state and local governments in raising their $6 billion, the federal government would establish an environmental financing authority that would float its own securities and use the proceeds to buy state and local waste treatment construction bonds. In addition federally aided plants would be required to meet prescribed operating and maintenance standards.

Is this enough money in face of the needs? There is no open-and-shut answer. With respect to municipal treatment works, the 1968 report of the Federal Water Pollution Control Agency ("The Cost of Clean Water") suggests the need, over a five-year period, for $8 billion in construction. At prices likely to prevail in the next five years, the cost would be nearer $9 billion to $10 billion. However, the FWPCA report also suggests the need for $6 billion in sanitary sewer construction. It points to the problem of combined storm and sanitary sewers (overflows during heavy rains bypass waste treatment plants and dump raw sewage into the river). While the costs—and even the best methods—of dealing with this problem are still very uncertain, they range from a minimum of $15 billion to a high of $45 billion. Additional costs would be required to control erosion from streambeds, roadways, and urban construction sites, to abate acid drainage from mines, and to control oil spills. By no means all of these costs will, or should, be borne by the federal government. But public authorities of some kind will have to bear some of the costs and require industry to bear others, if the problems are to be tackled. On balance it would appear that the combined federal, state, and local program proposed by the President is large enough to accommodate a fairly ambitious goal for the construction of municipal waste treatment facilities. But other needs are also emerging; the federal government will soon have to choose whether to make financial contributions to their fulfillment and, if so, how much.

RIVER BASIN PLANNING. The President proposes to require comprehensive river basin programs for pollution control by administrative actions. In addition communities will be "encouraged" to cooperate in the construction of large regional treatment plants, which are more efficient than a number of small municipal plants.

The obstacle to the imposition of system criteria is that they will, as noted earlier, affect the communities along a river basin in diverse ways. Politically, therefore, it may be very difficult to translate river basin plans into priority criteria for grant allocation and construction of treatment plants. Basin-wide user charges for pollution control might neutralize some of the political problems, since different treatment requirements would no longer be reflected in differential tax burdens. Federally sponsored river basin agreements among states and localities to establish common user charges might be considered as an adjunct to the President's emphasis on river basin planning.

INDUSTRIAL POLLUTION. The President's proposals call for the extension of federal water quality standards to intrastate waters. His proposed amendments seek to toughen enforcement by making standards much more specific than they are now and by prescribing fines of up to $10,000 a day for violators.

Effluent charges developed under federal criteria and imposed on industries in each river basin constitute a possible substitute for, or even addition to, judicial sanctions. The technique is relatively new in this country and requires sophistication in the setting of charges. On the other hand, it avoids the all-or-nothing showdown of a court case and maintains the courts as appellate tribunals rather than imposing upon them an administrative role in the complex process of limiting pollution.

Air Pollution Control

Airborne solids and gases pose a national problem in the form of direct damage to various kinds of materials, hazardous reductions in visibility, probable damage to human health, and the sheer unpleasantness of smog. The National Air Pollution Control Administration, established in 1967, is the principal federal agency with responsibilities in this field. Its activities consist mainly of making research outlays and grants to state and local pollution control organizations in support of their programs to set and enforce standards. Expenditures for these purposes will increase from $59 million in 1969 to $80 million and $104 million in 1970 and 1971, respectively.

The President's air pollution proposals have two major elements. First, the administration will issue new and more stringent standards controlling automobile pollution, to take effect partly in 1973 and partly in 1975, and new standards controlling gasoline additives (principally lead). Second, as in the case of water pollution, federal authority to set air quality standards will be extended and enforcement powers strengthened. National standards will be established and the states given one year to prepare abatement plans to meet them. States may establish more stringent standards if they wish.

Air pollution comes primarily from combustion, usually to produce energy but also to dispose of unwanted materials. It arises from a large number of small sources and is thus less amenable than water pollution to being collected and channeled for centralized processing, except in the case of industrial plants. Aside from municipal trash disposal, programs analogous to waste treatment facility grants are not required. Since most air pollution is caused by industrial, commercial, and private activities, its control depends on the setting of standards for private pollution discharges and the provision of sanctions or incentives to ensure that those standards are observed. The central thrust of current policy to achieve this goal is the use of judicial sanctions. Alternatively, taxes could be levied according to use of "dirty" fuels (soft coal, diesel oil, and others), method of combustion, and the amount of pollutants put into the air. Since the sources of air pollution are so diverse, various combinations of incentives could be used.

Much less is known about air quality standards than about water quality standards. The effect of various forms of air pollution on the environment is a subject about which much more needs to be learned. As a consequence the setting and enforcement of air quality standards must be much more evolutionary and subject to greater change than is the case with water pollution. Continued large-scale research support is also critically important. It seems reasonable, therefore, that the 1971 budget devotes $62 million to air pollution research, more than half the funds spent on the entire program.

Law Enforcement
and Criminal Justice

The maintenance of public order always has been among the essential functions of government, but only in the late 1960s were federal law enforcement programs greatly expanded. In addition to the traditional criminal justice programs—the enforcement machinery behind federal laws, the courts, and the correctional institutions—the Congress authorized in 1965 and expanded in 1968 financial assistance to state and local governments to enable them to bolster their own law enforcement efforts. Recently the federal government has also undertaken major activities to combat organized crime, civil disorders, and the illegal use of drugs. Between 1969 and 1971, total federal expenditures for law enforcement and criminal justice will virtually double, from $658 million spent in 1969 to $1,257 million budgeted for 1971. (See Table 4-12.)

This steep climb in federal spending has been prompted by nationwide concern over the rising incidence of crime. (See Table 4-13.) During the 1960s, the number of serious crimes (the "index" crimes

**Table 4-12. Federal Law Enforcement Expenditures
by Major Program, Fiscal Years 1969–71**

Thousands of dollars

Program	1969 actual	1970 estimate	1971 proposed
Federal criminal law enforcement	356,225	427,624	472,823
Law enforcement support	53,739	138,224	236,638
Services for prevention of crime	47,780	103,785	186,841
Rehabilitation of offenders	105,382	135,937	177,324
Administration of criminal justice	68,538	89,542	110,451
Crime research and statistics	13,443	26,920	43,209
Planning and coordination of crime reduction programs	12,900	24,272	28,600
Reform of criminal laws	346	1,037	1,452
Total	658,353	947,341	1,257,338

Source: *Special Analyses, Budget of the United States, Fiscal Year 1971*, pp. 197–98.

Table 4-13. Incidence of Serious Crimes as Reported by the FBI, Various Calendar Years, 1962–68[a]

Year	*Number of reported crimes (thousands)*	*Biennial rate of increase (percent)*
1962	2,214	10
1964	2,755	24
1966	3,264	18
1968	4,467	37

Source: U.S. Department of Justice, Federal Bureau of Investigation, *Uniform Crime Reports for the United States—1968*, p. 59.
a. "Serious crimes," as used here, include the seven most common violent and property crimes.

tabulated in the FBI's Uniform Crime Reports) more than doubled, with the highest incidence and rates of increase occurring in the large urban centers. (See Table 4-14.) The reliability of these crime statistics has long been subject to debate. On the one hand, it is generally agreed that the number of crimes reported is lower than the number actually committed. On the other, it has been argued that part of the recent rise in the *reported* crime rate is due to improved police surveillance and more accurate reporting methods rather than to a real increase in the incidence of crime. Whatever the merits of the statistical debate, a sustained high crime rate probably will mean a continuing and growing federal role, both in the level of federal spending and the forms of federal involvement. The programs started in recent years will not soon be ended or curtailed; indeed, the amounts proposed in the President's budget appear to be a base for higher spending in the future.

Two major lines of attack on the problem of crime are available: social investment in education, housing, job training, and the like, designed to reduce the disadvantages that breed crime; and expendi-

Table 4-14. Incidence of Serious Crimes in the United States, by Area, Calendar Year 1968

Area	*Number of crimes (thousands)*	*Crime rate per 100,000 population*
Standard Metropolitan Statistical Areas	3,823	2,803
Other cities	349	1,358
Rural areas	294	780

Source: U.S. Department of Justice, Federal Bureau of Investigation, *Uniform Crime Reports for the United States—1968*, p. 58. See Table 4-12, note (a), for definition of serious crimes.

tures on improving the criminal justice system itself, to provide greater deterrence and more effective law enforcement. Unfortunately, all too little is known about the yield of specific programs of either type in reducing crime. This section does not attempt to evaluate the relative effectiveness of various approaches; rather, it deals with some specific issues in the use of federal funds to improve law enforcement. The issues that dominate congressional consideration of the 1971 law enforcement budget focus on three matters of policy and procedure: (1) How much money should be spent? (2) How should funds be channeled to state and local governments by the Law Enforcement Assistance Administration (LEAA)? (3) How should the funds be used?

How Much Should Be Spent?

The 1971 budget recommends increases in almost every category of anticrime spending as indicated in Table 4-12, with the total increase amounting to $310 million, or one-third more than is being spent in the current year. While the Justice Department accounts for approximately two-thirds of total law enforcement spending, more than a dozen other agencies have some share. The law enforcement budget of the Justice Department, which approaches $850 million, may well be raised above the level recommended by the President. In fact, leading congressmen have introduced legislation that would authorize much higher levels of spending for the Law Enforcement Assistance Administration. The President's budget calls for $480 million in LEAA funds, up from $268 million in 1970; but the spending alternatives proposed by some congressmen range from $650 million to $1 billion for 1971.

It is difficult to estimate how much LEAA money could be usefully pumped into state and local criminal justice systems. The easy tendency is to assume that higher spending will somehow mitigate the crime problem, particularly because there are no available indicators of what has been accomplished thus far with LEAA funds. Yet from the perspectives of state and local recipients, there is some question whether significantly higher federal grants could be profitably used unless there are changes in the LEAA program. All LEAA grants require matching contributions by the recipient governments, with the state-local share ranging from 10 percent (planning grants) to 50 percent (construction projects). Most grants require a 40 percent state-local contribution. If one assumes that the recipients will have to put up two dollars for every three dollars received from the federal government, the 1971 budget will place a $320 million burden on the states and localities. If the LEAA grants go as high as $1 billion (which is unlikely), the state-local share under current matching formulas would rise to approximately $670 million, of which almost $500 million would be a totally new cost.

Aside from the prevailing difficulty of raising money from their own sources, local governments are handicapped by two aspects of the LEAA program. First, local budgets often are enacted before the level of federal grants is known. Even if the Congress were to appropriate LEAA funds in a timely fashion before the fiscal year begins, the grants must pass through several time-consuming state and regional reviews before allocations are made to specific localities for specific purposes. Local governments have reported difficulty in finding matching funds months after their own budgets have been adopted.

Another problem relates to the provision of the 1968 Omnibus Crime Control and Safe Streets Act limiting the amount that can be spent for police salaries to no more than one-third of a grant. Inasmuch as personal services account for as much as 80–90 percent of local police budgets, local governments might not be able to develop productive uses for substantially larger funds received from LEAA. Accordingly, an enlargement of LEAA might have to be coupled with a relaxation of the salary limitation and changes in the administration of the program.

How Should the Funds Be Channeled?

Under the 1968 act, 85 percent of LEAA funds are allocated to state governments on the basis of population. The states, in turn, are obligated to pass at least three-fourths of these funds to their local governments. This provision stirred considerable controversy when it was enacted, and it is now provoking renewed debate within the Congress. The attorney general has proposed an extension of the LEAA program (the initial authorization expires June 30, 1970) with certain minor corrective modifications. The basic methods of allocation—block grants to the states coupled with a mandatory pass-through—would not be changed.

However, a tug-of-war (similar in many ways to the dispute over the revenue-sharing proposal) has developed between big-city mayors who want either direct federal assistance to local governments or greater local control over LEAA grants, and governors who prefer to continue the present arrangement that gives state planning agencies the dominant voice in distributing funds among local recipients. The cities charge that they have been short-changed in the allocation of funds, that state planning agencies are insensitive to the crime problems of urban governments, and that the LEAA program in some states is dominated by rural and suburban authorities, which receive disproportionate shares of the funds. City officials point to the fact that approximately 85 percent of all serious crimes are committed in metropolitan areas and that the crime rate in these areas is more than three times the rate in rural areas. They argue that the money should go where the crime is, not where the states want to allocate it. The cities also complain about red tape caused by the multilayered planning and review processes, and of the attendant delays and uncertainty in obtaining funds.

The states were given primary allocative authority because they are closer to the crime problem than the national government. It was hoped that block grants to states would avoid the creation of a new Washington bureaucracy and the political difficulties that would arise if the federal government had to approve each project for each town and city. Moreover, each state could develop its own comprehensive law enforcement scheme, and local governments would be encouraged to coordinate their separate crime control efforts.

As the LEAA program has been carried out, several factors have led to a more favorable allocation of funds to rural and suburban governments than might have occurred if the funds were distributed through project grants or by a formula that relates the distribution of grants to the incidence of crime. Some states have given each local government an equal share, regardless of population or crime rate; others have given each local unit a minimum grant, distributing only the remaining funds according to some assessment of need. States have tended to favor rural police forces that lack modern equipment and training, while big-city law enforcement agencies that already possess the equipment and do their own training have been dis-advantaged.

In extending the LEAA program, the Congress can choose among several alternatives:

1. Retain the present funding methods and thereby allow the states to determine the distribution of funds among local recipients. Within this framework, the Congress might write into the authorization its own view that the incidence of crime should be considered by the states when they allocate funds.

2. Modify the pass-through feature to require states to allocate funds in a manner that reflects population density, crime rates, and current law enforcement efforts by local governments. Each of these criteria would probably lead to an increase in the shares received by large urban governments.

3. Reduce the portion of LEAA funds allocated as block grants from 85 percent to some smaller share, and increase the percentage of funds allocated at the discretion of LEAA itself. The major share of the 15 percent currently distributed at the discretion of LEAA has been earmarked for urban crime areas.

4. Abandon block grants and convert the Law Enforcement Assistance Administration funds into project grants, with LEAA establishing rules and allocating funds in accordance with general guidelines promulgated by the Congress. LEAA funds would then be granted directly to local governments.

How Should the Funds Be Used?

The 1968 Crime Control Act specifies that wherever possible, priority should be given to combating organized crime and controlling civil riots. But it also authorizes the use of LEAA funds for training law enforcement officers, purchasing equipment, and other crime prevention uses. The largest allocations have been for the training of law enforcement officers, general police support, and the improvement of correctional programs.

Federal officials do not want LEAA funds to be used to alleviate pressures on local budgets; rather, they want these funds to generate higher aggregate state-local investments in law enforcement efforts. This is one reason why the limitation on the payment of police salaries was written into the 1968 law.

At present the federal government has only an incremental role in the total law enforcement effort. Federal-state-local spending on criminal justice systems probably will exceed $6 billion in 1970. By far the largest part of these funds must be supplied by the states and localities from their own sources. Unless federal law enforcement assistance is to be regarded as a form of general financial aid, its object should be to prod recipient governments to conduct programs and undertake expenditures that they otherwise could not attempt. Thus some form of federal specification of the ultimate use of the funds—even though it is phrased in general terms—would seem essential to preserve the additivity feature of the LEAA grants.

New federal undertakings to improve certain aspects of the criminal justice system can be expected in the future. In November 1969, President Nixon directed the attorney general to develop a ten-year plan for reforming the nation's correctional institutions. While the President did not request funds, his prison reform message pointed to many areas in which more ought to be done. A related area in which higher federal spending might be anticipated, either in the form of a new program or as part of LEAA's activities, is the rehabilitation of drug users—a costly task requiring facilities that are not widely available. To judge from current efforts, few states and localities have been able to mount an effective attack on the problem.

Farm Price Supports

Total net farm income last year was $16 billion. The average net income per farm was $5,470, up 96 percent from ten years ago or 60 percent when measured in dollars of constant purchasing power. Farmers also received $13 billion from nonfarm sources such as part-time work, dividends, and social security payments. Through its farm commodity programs the federal government is supporting farm income at an estimated budgetary cost of $4.5 billion a year in fiscal 1970 and 1971.

Existing Programs and Four Alternatives

The 1965 farm legislation authorizing most existing commodity support programs will expire this year and new legislation will have to be enacted. How the new law is written—and equally important, how it is administered—will have a significant impact on both future budgetary costs and farm incomes. After outlining the main characteristics of existing farm programs, this section will suggest what appear to be the realistic options open to the Congress in enacting new farm legislation and to the administration in carrying it out in subsequent years.

The analysis is devoted principally to feed grains, wheat, and cotton. About 200 million acres are planted to these crops each year, or approximately two-thirds of the country's total harvested acreage. The price and income support programs devoted to them normally account for more than three-fourths of total annual farm program expenditures and for about half the total outlays of the Department of Agriculture. The aggregate level of farm income is especially sensitive to changes in these programs; opportunities to make significant alterations in federal expenditure patterns by modifying the programs for other crops are limited.

The programs for feed grains, wheat, and cotton exist by authority granted in the Food and Agriculture Act of 1965. (Price supports for milk, soybeans, tobacco, peanuts, rice, and a group of minor products are provided under authority dating back to the Agricultural Adjustment Act of 1938 and the Agricultural Act of 1948, as amended.) Under the act of 1965, direct payments are made to farmers who agree to divert substantial acreage from the production of the principal crops. Prices are supported at levels geared to the world markets for grains and cotton, though elements of the old "parity price" formula remain in the law.

The payments to farmers play two roles in supporting farm income. They directly increase income. And by inducing farmers to participate in the acreage diversion programs, they make it possible to manage supplies of farm products to keep production in line with demand. As a consequence, price support levels can be maintained without large-scale government buying and storage of farm commodities.

In considering farm commodity policies for the 1970s, four broad alternatives seem feasible:

1. Continue the administrative machinery of the existing law and the price support levels in effect for the 1969 and 1970 crops.

2. Amend the 1965 act to increase the price support levels for feed grains, to increase direct Treasury payments to wheat producers, to

authorize direct payments and an acreage diversion program for soybeans, and to establish a reserve of stored commodities as insurance against natural disasters affecting crop production. This is the proposal put forward in 1969 by eighteen general farm organizations and commodity groups known as the Farm Coalition.

3. Continue the basic provisions of the 1965 act but modify them to give the secretary of agriculture greater discretion in setting payments under the cotton and wheat programs. (Such discretion already exists for the feed grains program.) Use the discretionary authority to reduce payments gradually for cotton and wheat while lowering feed grain prices.

4. Adopt the approach outlined in (3) above, but in addition modify the existing law to give farm producers, within overall acreage restrictions, much more freedom to shift production from one major crop to another. This is the essence of the administration's proposed farm bill, recently submitted to the Congress.

Table 4-15 summarizes the budgetary consequences of these alternatives, each of which is explained in more detail below. By 1975 the alternatives range from an increase of $2 billion above current costs to a decrease of more than $1.5 billion. The spread between the high and the low options exceeds $3.5 billion.

Table 4-15. Estimates of Direct Payments to Farmers for Major Crops under Four Alternative Farm Programs, Fiscal Years 1971, 1973, and 1975

Millions of dollars

Alternative program	1971	1973	1975
Option 1: Current program, current price support levels	2,850	3,140	3,430
Option 2: Farm Coalition bill	2,850	4,450	4,900
Option 3: Greater discretionary authority[a]			
Wheat, cotton, and feed grain payments reduced	2,850	2,130	1,330
Wheat and cotton payments reduced; feed grain payments held constant	2,850	2,450	1,975
Option 4: Administration bill plus Option 3 discretionary authority[a]			
Wheat, cotton, and feed grain payments reduced	2,850	2,130	1,330
Wheat and cotton payments reduced; feed grain payments held constant	2,850	2,450	1,975

Source: Calculated from data presented in Tables 4-17, 4-18, 4-19, and 4-20.

a. Payments under Options 3 and 4 could be reduced by equal amounts, but farm incomes would be more severely affected by reduced payments under Option 4 than under Option 3. See text.

Clearly, the choices to be made in the legislation this year, and in its administration in subsequent years, will have an important impact on the allocation of budgetary resources. Those alternatives that would raise budgetary costs would also provide more income to farmers. Conversely, the lower cost programs are associated with some decrease in farm income. In addition to higher budgetary outlays, the Farm Coalition bill envisages an increase in the prices of feed grain and soybeans. As a consequence, the added costs would be shared by consumers and taxpayers.

Any of the four approaches offers the additional possibility of providing a limitation on the maximum payments that any one farmer could receive from the government. Such a limitation was approved by the House of Representatives in 1969 but rejected by the Senate. Payment limitation would further reduce budgetary costs. With costs at the $3 billion level, payment limitation could save from $200 million to $500 million a year, depending on the particular limits chosen and the effectiveness of program administration in preventing evasion of the limits.

Option 1: Continue the Existing Program

The four-year Food and Agriculture Act of 1965 (extended for one year in 1968) included discretionary features that gave the secretary of agriculture adequate authority to keep production of grain and cotton in line with demand and to dispose of surpluses. Federal funds were provided through arrangements that exempted them from normal appropriations procedures. The act also included discretionary authority that enabled the secretary to adjust the level at which market prices for various commodities were supported (loan rates). This authority is adequate to maintain appropriate relationships among commodities and to keep U.S. prices competitive in international markets. It has not been fully used.

For cotton a statutory provision has had the effect of requiring that any change in the level of market price supports (loan rates) be offset by a compensating change in payments to cotton farmers. This provision requires that the loan rate plus the price support payment to cotton farmers be equivalent to 65 percent of the parity price on an amount of cotton equal to 65 percent of production on the national acreage allotment. Administrators are understandably reluctant to reduce the cotton loan rate to maintain competitive prices when higher Treasury payments are an automatic result.

The 1965 act also included payment formulas for cotton and wheat that virtually insure that direct payments under those programs will increase year after year. These formulas gear total payments to parity prices, which are tied to the prices farmers pay for goods and services but which do not take into account rapidly increasing productivity on the farm. As prices paid by farmers for production and consumption items increase, parity prices increase and direct payments to cotton and wheat producers must also rise.

If the 1965 act were continued, federal cotton payments, now $900 million a year, would almost certainly escalate by an average of $30–$40 million a year. Federal payments to wheat producers would rise by approximately $30 million a year in response to a mandatory increase of an estimated 6 cents a bushel in parity-based Treasury payments on 500 million bushels of wheat.

More important, serious inequities among commodities and regions would be perpetuated if the 1965 act were continued without major amendments. The fixed statutory payment formulas for cotton and wheat *require* sizable income subsidies to producers of cotton and wheat over and above the amounts necessary to induce farmers to restrict their planted acreage. But the discretion given to the secretary of agriculture in the payment formula for feed grains, coupled with the powerful competition for federal funds, has denied large income subsidies to feed grain producers.

The effects of these differences in payment formulas are illustrated in Table 4-16, which uses 1968 data, made available last year by the Department of Agriculture, to distinguish the "supply management"

Table 4-16. Supply Management and Income Subsidy Payments to Farmers for Major Crops, Calendar Year 1968

Millions of dollars

Crop	Supply management payments		Income subsidy payments		Total payments
	Amount	Percentage of total	Amount	Percentage of total	
Wheat	384	51	362	49	746
Cotton	276	35	508	65	784
Feed grains	1,221	89	148	11	1,369
Total	1,881	65	1,018	35	2,899

Source: Walter E. Wilcox, *Economic Aspects of Farm Program Payment Limitations*, Library of Congress, Legislative Reference Service (Nov. 6, 1969), p. 1.

and "income subsidy" functions of direct federal payments in 1968. Supply management payments are the amount required in any year to balance supply and demand and thereby keep prices at or near support levels. The rest of the payments are classified as a direct income subsidy. While only 11 percent of feed grain payments were direct income subsidies in excess of the amount necessary to balance supply and demand at world market prices, 65 percent of cotton payments and 49 percent of wheat payments were direct income subsidies.

The budgetary costs of simply extending the 1965 act without material amendment are shown in Table 4-17. They are based on assumptions (1) that acreage diversion requirements will be set to balance supply and demand and that the Commodity Credit Corporation will not add to its commodity stocks, and (2) that rising parity prices will increase direct payments to wheat farmers by $30 million a year and to cotton growers by $36 million a year.

Aggregate gross and net farm income under option 1 would continue at or near recent levels. Income per farm would continue to increase as the number of farms declines along the recent trend line.

Option 2: The Farm Coalition Bill

Some twenty-seven farm organizations and commodity associations now jointly support a continuation of the Food and Agriculture Act of

Table 4-17. Direct Payments to Farmers for Wheat, Cotton, and Feed Grains, Fiscal Years 1968–71; and Projected Payments under Option 1 (Current Program, Current Price Support Levels), Fiscal Years 1973 and 1975[a]

Millions of dollars

Fiscal year	Wheat[b]	Cotton[c]	Feed grains[d]
1968	342	855	832
1969	359	736	1,427
1970	398	814	1,269
1971	430	902	1,516
1973	490	974	1,676
1975	550	1,046	1,836

Source: Analysis by John A. Schnittker, Kansas State University.

a. Figures for fiscal 1968 and 1969 are actual; those for other years are estimates or projections.

b. Based on estimated increases of 6 cents a year in the parity price for wheat. This would lead to a mandatory increase of 6 cents a bushel in Treasury-financed payments on about 500 million bushels of wheat each year.

c. Based on estimated increase of 1 cent a year in the parity price of cotton. The statutory payment formula would require an increase of about ⅔ cent a pound, or $3.33 a bale, in payments on 11 million bales of cotton each year.

d. Based on estimated increase of 2 million acres diverted from feed grains each year after 1970, to avoid an accumulation of surplus feed grains, for a payment of $40 an acre.

1965, with four important and budget-related amendments. The amendments would further reduce executive discretion in administering the farm programs, would insure higher annual payments to farmers, and would result in higher Treasury costs. Specifically, the coalition amendments would have the following effects:

1. Increase the level of the price support loan for corn to a minimum of $1.15 a bushel (for No. 2 grade), compared with the loan level of $1.05 in effect for several years.

2. Increase payments to wheat producers by requiring that the price support loan for wheat, plus payments on export wheat, be equal to at least 65 percent of the parity price.

3. Authorize Treasury payments to soybean producers for the first time and fix a minimum national average level of $2.75 a bushel for the combination of market price supports (loan rate) plus payments. The soybean support price is currently $2.25 a bushel. A new acreage diversion program would be authorized when soybean carryover exceeded 150 million bushels.

4. Authorize the secretary of agriculture to maintain a reserve of certain agricultural commodities and to dispose of such reserves only under conditions rigidly specified in the law. This would tend to increase the cost of most commodity price supports, but no specific estimates can be made for such a complex program. Because these amendments tend to encourage an expansion of farm output while decreasing the consumption of farm commodities, greater acreage diversion (smaller acreage allotments) would be required to avoid an accumulation of surplus feed grains and wheat under this option. The programs would be administratively manageable, however, if large additional amounts of money were available.

The budgetary costs are shown in Table 4-18 (the figures are directly comparable to those in Table 4-17). Key factors leading to changes in the program costs would be:

1. A marked increase in payments under the feed grain program resulting from price support incentives to farmers that were set about 10 percent higher than in 1969–70.

2. A sharp rise in the acreage that would have to be diverted from feed grains to prevent an accumulation of carryover stocks. This would be the direct outcome of increased yields per acre and lower total feed grain consumption resulting from higher market prices.

3. A new payment item of $385–$455 million a year for soybeans. This large new expenditure could not be avoided or materially re-

Table 4-18. Projected Direct Payments to Farmers for Wheat, Cotton, Feed Grains, and Soybeans under Option 2 (the Farm Coalition Bill), Fiscal Years 1971, 1973, and 1975

Millions of dollars

Fiscal year	Wheat[a]	Cotton[b]	Feed grains[c]	Soybeans[d]
1971	430	902	1,516	...
1973	837	974	2,256	385
1975	911	1,046	2,496	455

Source: Same as Table 4-17.

a. Based on Table 4-17, plus payments ranging from 60 to 84 cents a bushel (as parity price increases) on 520 million bushels of export wheat each year.

b. No changes from assumptions listed in Table 4-17.

c. Assumes a one-third increase in price support payment levels as required under the proposed program and (to offset higher farm price guarantees) a cumulative increase of 1 million acres diverted each year beyond the increase assumed in Table 4-17, in order to avoid an accumulation of surplus feed grains.

d. Assumes that payments range from 50 cents to 70 cents a bushel (as the parity price increases) on 700 million bushels of soybeans each year, and that about two-thirds of the crop is grown on complying farms.

duced under the language of the bill. It would include a large income subsidy, as distinguished from production adjustment payments.

The principal long-term result of adopting these amendments would be to increase the imbalance between potential agricultural production and expected utilization of U.S.-produced agricultural commodities in any year. Keeping this additional productive capacity in check by means of voluntary, payment-based production control programs would be the source of the greater costs.

Gains in aggregate farm income would be greater in any year than the increase in direct payments to farmers, since market prices for feed grains would be 10 percent higher and livestock prices would increase as feed costs increase.

Option 3: Greater Discretionary Authority under the 1965 Act

Increased discretion logically would apply to those aspects of farm programs that are now fixed by statute and that have important fiscal or farm income implications. Cotton and wheat payment formulas and large payments to individual farmers stand out in this category.

Two guiding purposes of amendments to the 1965 act and subsequent administrative actions could be, first, to bring the total level of payments in any year under the control of the President and the secretary of agriculture, rather than allowing them to flow automatically from statutory requirements. This would bring decisions on the level of farm payments into competition with priority programs in areas other than agriculture. It would not require reductions in commodity spending but would make such reductions possible. Second, direct income subsidies could be gradually confined to low-income farmers, thereby gearing most direct farm payments after a few years to the levels required to adjust production to demand. In effect this would make payments under the cotton and wheat programs serve the same supply management functions that are served by payments under the feed grain program.

A reduction in cotton and wheat payments over five years is illustrated in Table 4-19. The payments would remain large enough to keep supplies in line with consumption, with cotton payments financed by the Treasury and wheat payments out of consumer budgets through a continuation of the existing wheat certificate levels. By 1975, Treasury-financed payments in these programs would be $800 million smaller than in 1971 and about at the levels intended when the Food and Agriculture Act of 1965 was originally submitted to the Congress.

Increasing yields of feed grains are expected to outrun the growth of demand. Barring reductions in price support levels, feed grain payments would increase according to the pattern shown in Table 4-17, even while cotton and wheat payments were being reduced. If feed grain payments were to be fixed at the 1971 level through 1975, or if they were to be lowered, market price supports would have to be reduced rather sharply. Such a result is illustrated by two options in Table 4-20. The numbers are very rough estimates, but the direction of change seems certain.

Table 4-19. Projected Direct Payments to Farmers for Wheat and Cotton under Option 3 (Greater Discretionary Authority), Fiscal Years 1971, 1973, and 1975

Millions of dollars

	Wheat			
Fiscal year	Financed by consumer[a]	Financed by Treasury	Total	Cotton
1971	397	430	827	902
1973	400	230	630	700
1975	400	30	430	500

Source: Same as Table 4-17.
a. Total consumption of wheat-based foods, principally flour, has been rising slightly in recent years. Hence these payments may increase somewhat, since they are tied to grindings of wheat to be used as human food in the United States.

Table 4-20. Projected Direct Payments to Farmers for Feed Grains and Acreage Diversions under Option 3 (Greater Discretionary Authority), Fiscal Years 1971, 1973, and 1975

	Fiscal 1971 payment level held constant			Fiscal 1971 payment level reduced		
Fiscal year	Payments (millions)	Corn loan (per bushel)	Acres diverted[a] (millions)	Payments (millions)	Corn loan (per bushel)	Acres diverted[a] (millions)
1971	$1,516	$1.05	38	$1,516	$1.05	38
1973	1,516	1.01	38	1,200	0.95	30
1975	1,516	0.97	38	800	0.85	22

Source: Same as Table 4-17.

a. Under option 2 (the Farm Coalition bill), 44 million acres would be diverted in 1973 and 50 million in 1975. Extension of current price support levels would require the diversion of 42 million and 46 million acres, respectively.

Option 4: The Administration Bill

The administration's farm proposals were submitted to the agriculture committees of the Congress on February 3. They would continue the existing system of direct payments to farmers as a means of inducing them to divert acreage for supply management purposes. However, they incorporate a number of changes. First, as in option 3, the secretary of agriculture would have wide discretion in setting payment levels, but the *upper* limits of the new formulas for cotton and wheat would be no higher than the statutory minimum now provided. Second, the range in which price supports could be offered for feed grains and wheat would be broadened. Third, a significant change would be made in the technique by which farm acreage is diverted. In exchange for direct payments, farmers would agree in effect to an overall acreage "set-aside." On the remainder of their tillable acreage they could plant any combination of crops, without regard to prior crop history. Finally, the bill would require that funds for farm price supports and program payments be appropriated or authorized in advance, ending the present "backdoor financing" procedures that make funds automatically available without prior appropriations action.

The bill provides for more administrative discretion than any comprehensive farm law ever enacted. Although the bill may allow more discretion than a secretary of agriculture could put to practical use, somewhat more is clearly essential for fiscal management and the freedom of action compatible with today's competition for public funds. The bill would not assure either higher or lower spending for farm commodity programs, but it would provide a basis for either.

Secretary Clifford M. Hardin has indicated that no immediate or drastic changes are planned in program operations under the proposed authority and that recent cost levels will be maintained for a time. However, the administration is expected eventually to use the broad discretion in the proposed program to reduce farm spending or to prevent increases where possible. In considering the administration program, it is assumed here that (1) the program will be operated in the first year (crop year 1971, fiscal year 1972) with price supports for major commodities set at approximately the same levels as in fiscal 1970 and 1971; and that (2) price support and program payments will be reduced beginning with the 1972 crops and will show sizable reductions by crop year 1974 (fiscal year 1975).

For 1971–72, the main effect of the administration program would be to incur greater federal costs than does the present program to achieve a given level of gross and net farm income. Alternatively, to hold the line on program costs would reduce gross and net farm income. This would occur because some acreage now withheld from the production of major crops by the rather stringent requirements of present law would become eligible to produce those crops on participating farms under the more flexible requirements of the set-aside. This has commonly been called "slippage." Because of slippage,

Table 4-21. Comparison of Farm Income under Current Farm Price Support Program and Set-Aside Program, 1971

Millions of dollars

Type of income	Program of 1969 type, 1971	Set-aside program, 1971
Total gross income from production of wheat, cotton, feed grains, and soybeans	12,733	11,850
Less: Production costs (average of $34 per acre)	7,582	7,752
Net income	5,151	4,098
Income generated by setting aside other crops[a]	0	492
Total net farm income	5,151	4,590
Value of government payments[b]	3,162	3,162

Source: Luther Tweeten, "An Economic Appraisal of the Set-Aside Proposal," paper presented at a seminar sponsored by the Iowa Center for Agricultural and Economic Development in St. Louis, Jan. 29–30, 1970.

a. Computed as follows: The 15 million acre set-aside of other crops, corrected for slippage, is assumed to reduce by 12 million acres the production of other crops valued at $26 per acre. The total value is $312 million, or 0.69 percent of farm output. Since each 1 percent decrease in farm output has been estimated to raise net farm income 6 percent, 0.69 percent raises net farm income by 4.1 percent. If net income (excluding government payments) is $12 billion, the increase is 0.041 ($12 billion), or $492 million.

b. Includes the portion of wheat payments paid by processors.

greater budgetary costs are required to meet a given supply management objective—or lower prices and incomes are necessary if budgetary costs are held constant. (See Table 4-21.)

The advantage of the set-aside is that it gives farmers greater flexibility to switch cropping patterns. Its disadvantage, arising from the slippage factor, is that it requires higher budgetary costs to meet any given farm income objective, or conversely, that it results in lower farm incomes for any given set of budgetary costs.

For the 1975 crop year, it is assumed that the administration program is operated in much the same fashion as shown in the preceding tables on option 3. Wheat, cotton, and feed grain payments would be reduced by the amounts shown in those tables. Such a reduction in payments, totaling $1.5 billion, would reduce gross farm income by more than $2 billion below what it would have been without cuts in program payments. The option 3 payment cuts would also reduce gross incomes, but by a somewhat smaller amount.

Limiting Payments per Farm

Department of Agriculture statistics on direct government payments in 1968 show that 50 percent of the payments went to the 9 percent of farmers receiving the largest sums, and that fully one-quarter of the payments went to the upper 2 percent. Such information has prompted several congressmen to introduce legislation that would limit the size of payments to individual farms.

A $20,000 limit on *total direct payments to any producer* (the Conte-Findley amendment) was approved by the House of Representatives in 1968 and 1969 and is a ranking possibility for adoption in 1970. A limit of $10,000 *per producer per crop* (the Goodell amendment) was defeated in the Senate in 1969. The latter approach would be less troublesome administratively. A limit of $5,000 per producer per crop, proposed to the House Committee on Agriculture by Congressman Conte, appears to be the lowest feasible limit. The administration bill includes a complex graduated scale that would affect only a small number of farmers.

All of these proposals apply only to cotton, wheat, and feed grains. Payments under the Sugar Act and Wool Act could be covered by the same formula if the principle of limitation is adopted by the Congress.

Assuming total farm payment levels about equal to those of 1969–

70, the annual payment reductions under the three approaches examined in detail below might be as follows:

Conte-Findley ($20,000 per farm)	$180 million
Goodell ($10,000 per program)	$250 million
Conte ($5,000 per program)	$493 million

These figures would be measurably increased if sugar and wool were included. The administration proposal would save much smaller sums.

At the lowest level ($5,000), a substantial part of the $493 million payment reduction might be lost through farm splitting to avoid the limitations. In addition, some of the savings would have to be paid to other, smaller feed-grain producers and wheat farmers in order to meet supply management and stabilization goals that could be partially compromised when large-scale farmers no longer participate fully in the acreage diversion program. However, most of the payment reductions noted above *could* be net savings under any of these options, given appropriate statutory language and administrative regulations to control evasion.

The Conte-Findley amendment.[3] This proposal, placing a ceiling of $20,000 on total payments to any farmer, would have affected about 10,000 producers of cotton, wheat, and feed grains who received payments totaling some $380 million in 1968. The ceiling would have reduced this total to $200 million and yielded savings to the government of $180 million a year.

The Goodell amendment. Senator Goodell has proposed to limit farmers to a payment of $10,000 for any given crop. In 1968 the limit would have applied to some 25,386 farmers—15,097 cotton producers, 5,428 feed grain producers, and 4,861 wheat growers. Their payments would have been reduced by half, from about $515 million to $265 million.

The amendment would permit various acreage adjustments as a measure of equity. Large-scale grain producers whose payments were limited would be allowed to plant additional acres in proportion to their payment reductions. They would be given the same incentive to enroll in voluntary adjustment programs as smaller producers whose payments were not affected by the limitation. Cotton growers would be allowed to plant more than their allotment, up to a specified point, without incurring marketing penalties. The latter provision would probably not result in large increases in cotton production because most cotton growers would not increase their acreage at prevailing world prices.

The Conte proposal to the House Agriculture Committee. This proposal is similar to the Goodell amendment, though it would set a ceiling of $5,000 instead of $10,000 per crop. In 1968 it would have affected some 85,000 farmers by reducing their total payments from $917 million to $424 million. If the Conte proposal allowed the same equity adjustments as the Goodell amendment, the acreage diversion for feed grain and wheat would have been reduced by only some 7 percent and 10 percent, respectively. It is worth noting that 92 percent of the cotton growers, 97 percent of the wheat producers, and 98 percent of the feed grain producers would not have been affected by a $5,000 payment limit in 1968.

Space

Budgeting for the exploration of space and associated technology presents the President with a paradox. On the one hand, it may be argued that these expenditures, despite their practical scientific and technical yield, are more heavily dependent than others upon his sense of the value Americans place on an intangible: the satisfaction of an age-old spirit of adventure which, though impossible to measure, has been the driving force behind much of what we call progress. This is an objective somewhat apart from the concern for the material well-being and physical security of the citizenry that animates most government activities. The space program, it might be concluded, offers the archetype of the controllable expenditure that can be regulated entirely according to current needs and priorities.

On the other hand, there are powerful practical limits to this apparent flexibility. Major space projects are immense undertakings that require assembling and training highly specialized teams of technical people on a scale of time, expense, and precision almost unrivaled in history. Decisions on major objectives normally are expressed in action programs extending over many years (and several administrations), and not only establish claims to future financial resources but also divert skilled manpower in a number of important fields. Moreover, the capacity to build on past achievements with increasing efficiency and dispatch depends in large part on maintaining the motivation and involvement of experienced people, which in turn rests on the momentum of the program and the technical attractions it offers.

Pressed by powerful forces on all sides of the question of the proper position of space activities among national priorities, the President must try to choose an acceptable course toward goals that will largely be achieved near the end of the decade or later and that will greatly condition American efforts to explore the heavens through the end of the century. The budget estimates suggest that there has been a thoroughgoing examination of the issues, leading to selection of a policy with the following major characteristics:

- Lesser status for space programs vis-à-vis other federal activities than prevailed in the 1960s. In particular, no dramatic new goal for manned planetary exploration during the current decade.
- Greater priority within the program for activities designed to advance scientific knowledge and yield practical benefits, as compared with manned flight and exploration. This was made even clearer by the President's message to the Congress on space, dispatched on March 8, which stressed unmanned "grand tour" flybys of the outer planets in the late seventies or early eighties.
- Emphasis within manned flight activities upon perfecting the capacity to live and work in space, as well as to service space stations with reusable shuttle rockets. This is intended as preparation for planetary travel, apparently beginning with Mars, expected to be undertaken in later decades.

Trends and Options

The space budget in the 1960s was dominated by the requirements of the manned lunar landing program. Thus, as shown in Table 4-22, even though spending for other purposes stayed approximately level for the last five years of the decade, the pattern of expenditures over the ten years shows a rapid increase to a peak near $6 billion in the middle years followed by a decline to the proposed 1971 level of $3.4 billion. This trend reflects the high initial costs of establishing facilities for manufacturing and launching vehicles, followed by a tailing off to the somewhat lower costs of actually building and using them.

Table 4-22. Federal Outlays for Space Research and Technology, Various Fiscal Years, 1960–71

Millions of dollars

	Actual					Estimate	
Category	1960	1962	1964	1966	1968	1970	1971
Lunar program	113	565	2,768	4,210	3,096	1,868	1,254
Other programs	288	692	1,402	1,723	1,625	2,018	2,146
Total	401	1,257	4,170	5,933	4,721	3,886	3,400

Source: *The Budget of the United States Government, Fiscal Year 1971*, pp. 98, 587.

The staggering success of the national commitment to land a man on the moon and bring him back safely during the 1960s confronted the President with a set of policy alternatives in some ways even more difficult than that he would have faced if the lunar project had lagged. Not only had the Apollo program accomplished its goal, but it also produced technical capacity and potential sufficient to support substantial further progress in several different directions at rates of speed dependent, within broad limits, almost solely on the level of financial support. Moreover, it was reasonably clear that the only way to reduce the space budget significantly below $3 billion a year was to abandon manned space flight operations. If the physical and human resources created for Apollo were to be put to any use and further developed, the real range of choice was limited to the proper size of increases above that level.

To assist him with these issues, the President appointed in February 1969 a space task group, headed by the Vice President, which delivered its recommendations in September of that year. The group emphasized three options, all of them lower than the maximum pace that technology would allow, but all asserting the desirability of a substantial manned flight element. Table 4-23 shows the budget implications extended over the decade. The high option (1) would involve a fairly steady increase to about $9.5 billion; the middle option (2) grows more slowly to $7.7 billion; and the low option (3) grows as fast as the middle one through 1977 but flattens out at $5.5 billion a year thereafter.

All of these options refer to the same range of possible projects. As shown in Table 4-24, the difference lies solely in the timing of completion, and the only difference between options 2 and 3 is that the

Table 4-23. Expenditures under NASA Task Group Options, Fiscal Years 1970–80

Millions of dollars

Year	Option 1	Option 2	Option 3
1970	3,900	3,900	3,900
1971	4,250	3,950	3,950
1972	4,850	4,050	4,050
1973	5,850	4,250	4,250
1974	6,800	5,000	5,000
1975	7,700	5,450	5,450
1976	8,250	5,500	5,500
1977	8,750	5,500	5,500
1978	9,100	5,650	5,500
1979	9,350	6,600	5,500
1980	9,400	7,650	5,500

Source: *The Post-Apollo Space Program: Directions for the Future,* Space Task Group Report to the President (September 1969), p. 22.

former projects a manned mission to Mars by 1986 and the latter leaves the issue open. In other words, between now and 1977 options 2 and 3 are the same.

The task group also identified another option in which manned space flight was abandoned altogether but scientific programs and practical applications were pursued at the maximum rate. This option was not costed out in detail, but was presumed to "reduce gradually to a sustaining level of $2–3 billion depending on the depth of change assumed for the supporting NASA facilities and manpower base."[4]

This maze of alternatives, in the tight budgetary context outlined in previous chapters, would seem to have presented the President with three broad choices:

• Phase out manned flight for the next decade, concentrating on early and relatively low-cost achievement of scientific and practical objectives.

• Try to maintain Apollo-level momentum with an ambitious manned flight program with a specific date for the first mission to Mars.

• Retain manned flight capability; reduce investment in manned projects to the minimum consistent with preserving the NASA team and its motivation to develop the capabilities for planetary flight against the day when financial conditions are again conducive to such huge undertakings.

Table 4-24. Timing of NASA Task Group Programs

Program and objective	Year in which objective is to be achieved		
	Maximum pace	Option 1	Options 2 and 3
Manned systems:			
Space station, earth orbit	1975	1976	1977
50-man space base, earth orbit	1980	1980	1984
100-man space base, earth orbit	1985	1985	1989
Lunar orbiting station	1976	1978	1981
Lunar surface base	1978	1980	1983
Initial Mars expedition	1981	1983	1986ᵃ
Space transportation system:			
Earth-to-orbit shuttle	1975	1976	1977
Nuclear orbit transfer stage	1978	1978	1981
Space tug	1976	1978	1981
Scientific programs:			
Large orbiting observatory	1979	1979	1980
High-energy astronomical capability	1973	1973	1981
Out-of-ecliptic survey	1975	1975	1978
Mars high resolution mapping	1977	1977	1981
Venus atmospheric probes	1976	1976	mid-1980s
Multiple outer-planet "tours"	1977–79	1977–79	1977–79
Asteroid belt survey	1975	1975	1981
Applications:			
Earth resource system	1975	1975	1976
Direct broadcast demonstration	1978	1978	mid-1980s
Navigation and traffic-control demonstration	1974	1974	1976

Source: *The Post-Apollo Space Program: Directions for the Future*, Space Task Group Report to the President (September 1969), p. 20.
a. Under option 2. Under option 3, the year of completion is open.

Thrust of the 1971 Budget

The President, according to this budget and his space message, has apparently selected the third course—maintaining manned projects at or near the minimum necessary to sustain and improve the capability while pressing ahead with scientific projects and practical applications. Once this decision had been taken, the principal manned projects chosen to hold the interest and commitment of the NASA team, in addition to four more flights to the moon in 1971 and 1972, are the reusable earth-to-orbit shuttle system and the large earth-orbit space station designed for missions of up to fifty-six days. A manned landing on Mars is retained as a "longer-range" goal in the space message but is not attached to any target date, although the projects

Table 4-25. Budget Allocations for Various NASA Programs, Fiscal Years 1969–71

Percentages of total NASA budget allocations

Program	1969	1970	1971
Manned space flight	**56.1**	**52.7**	**44.2**
Apollo program	52.2	43.7	28.7
Other space flight operations[a]	3.9	9.0	15.5
Space science and its applications	**11.6**	**13.5**	**16.9**
Advanced research and technology	**7.2**	**7.1**	**8.0**
Nuclear rocket program	0.9	0.9	1.1
Aeronautical vehicle program	1.9	2.0	2.6
Other programs and activities	4.4	4.2	4.2

Source: *The Budget of the United States Government, Fiscal Year 1971—Appendix*, p. 825. Figures for sub-categories under advanced research and technology are estimates by Bruno W. Augenstein, The RAND Corporation.

a. Includes space station and earth-to-orbit shuttle.

listed above, as well as the planned development of nuclear rocket engines, are all applicable to manned planetary exploration. Among unmanned operations, emphasis is placed on the plan to send probes to every planet in the solar system during the 1970s and early 1980s, taking particular advantage of a rare "lineup" of the five outer planets toward the end of the period. Table 4-25 demonstrates the shift in priorities implied by the 1971 budget request.

While the 1971 budget reflects the President's basic decision to maintain a manned space flight capability, proposed expenditures are $500 million below the lowest manned space option presented by the task group. This difference is accounted for primarily by decisions to suspend additional production of the Saturn V launch vehicle and spacecraft used in the Apollo program, and to stretch out the current and planned start-up commitments in manned space flight. In planning for the lunar landing, NASA had long ago decided to procure fifteen Saturn V boosters, to have a reserve against program difficulties. The program has been so successful, however, that only seven boosters have been used, up through last November's second lunar landing. The administration has decided to stop production and use the remaining boosters in the existing inventory to fulfill lunar landing and Apollo application missions or as space station prototypes during the next several calendar years. If the suspension is brief, it could result in no appreciable break in capacity for manned flights; if it is extended, it would seem to ensure a hiatus of manned operations in the middle years of the 1970s, as well as ultimately to result in the idling of technical personnel and facilities assembled on the assumption that a high level of manned operations would continue indefinitely. An additional decision—deferral of the Viking unmanned landing on Mars scheduled for 1976—has been identified by the space message as a three-year delay to provide relatively minor current budgetary relief.

Perhaps most important, the 1971 budget does not appear to foreclose any major technological development currently of substantial interest. Although quite restrictive in some cases, it provides an array of future opportunities in that it will support continuation of current technological development and exploitation of existing capacity while also providing some of the building blocks necessary to initiate new development. It is a policy that does not concentrate on an all-out commitment to a single dramatic objective, but rather seeks to stimulate deliberate progress along a number of important fronts at the same time. If successful, it will not only promote several specific objectives but also permit effective holding actions in areas where overall budgetary constraints dictate against prompt investment of additional funds.

Main Issues in the 1971 Strategy

Many detailed questions are raised by the 1971 proposals, but two broad issues seem particularly critical to the success of the strategy they embody. The first question is whether the current set of objectives can maintain the aggressive enthusiasm that has contributed so handsomely to NASA's success. In the past this sense of mission and accomplishment has been closely linked to the focus on Apollo. It is legitimate to ask whether the smaller, less glamorous projects will, singly or together, command the same fascination from so many of the best minds in the relevant fields.

As a practical matter, and despite the great scientific value of the unmanned probes, the answer to this question will rest primarily on the importance attached to the space shuttle and station projects. On paper the technical problems in the shuttle alone should provide more than enough challenge, perhaps more than was provided by Apollo. Indeed, the difficulties may be even greater than suggested in the budget because in at least one important area—the information processing requirements connected with the desired reusability and rapid turnaround capability—the shuttle will demand performance well beyond that of past space systems. This will probably require a new generation of computer hardware and significant innovations in software, both of which will be of major scale but are as yet completely unspecified. This single item could amount to 15–25 percent of the total cost of developing the shuttle and, unless addressed with great vigor and originality, could push the entire vehicle into the late 1970s rather than 1976, the date for the first launch postulated in the space message.

Given these considerations, the current program probably contains the "critical mass" of technical challenge necessary to keep the NASA team engaged and infused with constant additions of new and high quality talent. There is, of course, always some element of gambling in predicting what will motivate human beings. But the budget proposals do provide a reasonable basis for rational persuasion. It remains to be seen how far the writ of reason runs.

The second main issue is whether the budget provides the basis—financial and political—for the adequate and orderly multiyear planning and funding its new emphases demand. For example, it may be that 1971 financing of the space shuttle, although increased from the previous year, is less than would be required by a firm commitment to achieve the capability within the current decade, let alone the 1976 objective mentioned in the message. Similarly, the budget does not make clear (though the message somewhat ambiguously affirms) that the shuttle and space station capacities are to be developed concurrently rather than sequentially.

Even more significant than these issues of scale, however, is the question of acceptance by both NASA and the Congress that realization of the full benefits of a broadly balanced program of technological development requires a multiyear commitment to minimize abortive stops and starts. Contrasted to a program built around a single overarching mission goal, this effort requires both a more complex review and planning process on the part of NASA and a correspondingly extended authority from the relevant sources of appropriations. Recognition of the former is implied by NASA's creation of a new post of director of planning at the level of associate administrator. His success, however, will depend heavily on the agency's (and the President's) ability to persuade the Congress to provide the continuity of financing necessary to give substance to such plans.

Table 4-26. Federal Obligations for Research and Development, Various Fiscal Years, 1955–71[a]

Millions of dollars

Department or agency	1955	1960	1965	1967	1968	1969	1970	1971
Grand total[b]	**2,749**	**8,062**	**15,709**	**16,723**	**16,472**	**16,164**	**16,357**	**15,810**
Total, excluding National Aeronautics and Space Administration[b]	**2,684**	**7,575**	**10,208**	**11,711**	**11,952**	**12,119**	**12,353**	**12,456**
Major agencies:								
Department of Defense	2,084	5,825	6,728	7,809	7,881	7,869	7,911	7,762
National Aeronautics and Space Administration	65	487	5,093	5,012	4,520	4,045	4,004	3,354
National Institutes of Health/National Institute of Mental Health	57	281	587	842	881	896	917	930
Atomic Energy Commission (weapons)	211	390	527	499	551	552	504	481
National Science Foundation	10	88	195	314	338	301	317	384
Subtotal	2,427	7,071	13,130	14,476	14,171	13,663	13,653	12,911
Other, primarily social, agencies:								
Department of Health, Education, and Welfare (excluding NIH/NIMH)	14	78	374	423	437	418	346	529
Department of Housing and Urban Development	...	...	...	11	15	18	34	60
Office of Economic Opportunity	...	...	4	47	43	35	68	90
Veterans Administration	6	19	43	48	48	53	61	65
Department of the Interior (water pollution control)	...	...	33	83	101	112	111	134
Department of Justice	...	...	...	3	1	6	13	29
Subtotal[c]	20	97	454	615	645	642	633	907
Other, primarily industrial, agencies:								
Atomic Energy Commission (excluding weapons)	162	598	994	980	981	1,155	1,217	1,078
Department of Transportation	...	53	99	106	124	129	204	226
Department of Agriculture	73	129	218	269	277	278	294	306
Department of Commerce	16	33	74	79	79	74	87	99
Department of the Interior (excluding water pollution control)	33	67	82	126	116	129	146	137
Subtotal	284	880	1,467	1,560	1,577	1,765	1,948	1,846
Addendum:								
Basic research (included in agency totals)	138	560	1,547	1,875	1,956	2,134	2,017	2,024

Source: Tabulations by John M. Deutch, Massachusetts Institute of Technology, on the basis of data from the *Special Analyses: Budget of the United States, Fiscal Year 1971*, and from publications of the National Science Foundation.

a. Includes obligations for research and development facilities.

b. Includes relatively minor research and development obligations of smaller agencies not listed below.

c. Since data on the research and development obligations of the Departments of the Interior and Justice are not available in all years, some small part of each annual change shown by these subtotals reflects changes in statistical coverage rather than changes in obligations.

Research and Development

In its proposed programs for research and development (R&D), the 1971 budget makes no dramatic departures from budgets of recent years. It calls for approximately $15.8 billion in support of scientific activities by government agencies, industrial firms, universities, and research centers. These expenditures are distributed among the programs of almost all the major federal agencies. However, five agencies —the Department of Defense (DOD), Atomic Energy Commission (AEC), National Institutes of Health (NIH), National Institute of Mental Health (NIMH), and the National Aeronautics and Space Administration (NASA)—continue to account for approximately 85 cents of every federal R&D dollar. Most of them will maintain their R&D efforts at approximately 1970 levels. The main exception is NASA, all of whose activities are classified as R&D and whose proposed obligations will decline by $650 million. Comparatively small but potentially significant increases are proposed for research related to several social and domestic programs, among the most notable being urban transportation, elementary education, law enforcement, pollution control, and housing. (See Table 4-26.)

Trends in R&D Expenditures

During the 1960s federal R&D activity more than doubled, from about $8 billion in fiscal 1960 to an estimated $16.4 billion in 1970. The rate of growth was highest during the 1955–64 period, followed by a very slow rise to 1967 and a modest decline thereafter. If NASA expenditures are excluded, federal commitments for R&D during the past three years have been nearly constant. But this stability quite probably masks a decrease in the volume of real resources devoted to R&D. Table 4-27 shows the results of applying alternative measures of price increases to these programs. The first assumes that the price of R&D rises equally with the average of other prices in the economy. The second assumes that movements in R&D prices are more closely represented by the movement in wage rates. The former method may understate and the latter overstate the decline in the volume of real resources applied.

Table 4-27. Obligations for Research and Development, in Constant Dollars, Fiscal Years 1967 and 1971

Millions of 1967 dollars

Expenditure category and deflation index	1967	1971
Total obligations, including NASA		
Deflated by a general price index[a]	16,723	13,490
Deflated by a nonfarm wage index[b]	16,723	12,265
Total obligations, excluding NASA		
Deflated by a general price index[a]	11,711	10,628
Deflated by a nonfarm wage index[b]	11,711	9,663

Source: Authors' estimates.
a. GNP deflator.
b. Private nonfarm compensation per manhour.

The decline in the real level of R&D is probably offset to some degree by increases in productivity arising from an accumulation of R&D capital in the form of equipment, facilities, trained personnel, and knowledge. The fall-off has resulted from a combination of only loosely related factors, inasmuch as federal R&D allocations are dispersed among the budgets of many agencies, and decisions in those agencies are made in relation to internal needs and constraints rather than in terms of an overall federal R&D policy. While R&D has been affected by the general tightness of the federal budget since 1968, it has also been buffeted by the spending experiences of the major suppliers of R&D funds, particularly DOD, NASA, and the Department of Health, Education, and Welfare (HEW).

Department of Defense

After rising fairly steadily from the mid-fifties to the mid-sixties, the Defense Department's R&D budget has fluctuated between $7.7 billion and $8.2 billion since 1967. Much of the growth in the early sixties was related to the buildup of strategic missile forces. Of total Defense R&D, approximately 80 percent is for development, 15 percent for applied research, and less than 5 percent for basic research. The major portion is channeled to a small number of high-cost strategic and tactical weapon systems. As long as the United States continues to pursue a vigorous program of new weapon systems development, DOD's expenditures are not likely to fall significantly.

It is difficult to estimate the consequences of a restriction in the 1970 military authorization bill that would limit the Defense Department's

R&D expenditures to activities that have a "direct and apparent relationship to a specific military function." Although some universities and institutes that rely heavily on DOD grants for support have expressed fear that this limitation will force them to terminate many important research projects, as yet there is no direct evidence of substantial cutbacks resulting from this prohibition. In his posture statement for fiscal 1971, Secretary Laird cautioned against "expecting significant budget reductions" as a consequence of the prohibition on nonmilitary research. He took the position that most Defense R&D programs are related to the department's mission and that as a result of cutbacks imposed on the 1970 budget, the department already had been compelled to pare its support of research.

National Institutes of Health and National Institute of Mental Health

After a long period of very rapid growth, the research budgets of NIH and NIMH began to level off in 1968. As constituent agencies of HEW, they have prospered or economized along with the parent department. In the late 1960s, HEW in general and the Institutes in particular were constrained by several budgetary developments. Congress enacted overall expenditure ceilings for both 1969 and 1970, and a sharp expansion in uncontrollable outlays consumed most of the growth permitted in total departmental expenditures. As a result, HEW was compelled to reduce the size and number of research grants made by the Institutes in order to keep within its expenditure allocation. These limitations have worked a special hardship on biomedical research because HEW, faced with mandatory cost increases in its Medicare and Medicaid programs, has favored health services over health research and development.

The experiences of the past several years, as exemplified by R&D spending patterns in the agencies examined here, suggest that national policy concerning R&D changed in the late 1960s. But these changes reflected not so much a deliberate attempt to modify government-wide R&D policy as shifts in particular federal programs to which R&D efforts are linked. The National Science Foundation (NSF) is an agency dedicated to the support of R&D for its own sake. But despite a requested $67 million increase in the NSF budget for 1971 (a 24 percent jump), the agency will still receive little more than 2 percent of the federal research dollar. Thus in the absence of a strong commitment to research on its own merits, it appears likely that major R&D must continue to ride the coattails of program support for specific federal missions.

Social Programs

Perhaps the most important feature of the R&D portions of the 1971 budget is the acceleration of increases in the efforts associated with numerous domestic social programs. While the total of such expenditures is still a relatively small fraction of federal R&D outlays, the 1971 budget proposes a significant increase. In HEW, for example, research and development obligations for agencies other than NIH and NIMH would rise from $346 million in fiscal 1970 to $529 million in 1971. In the Department of Housing and Urban Development (HUD) they would increase from $34 million to $60 million, and in the Office of Economic Opportunity (OEO) from $68 million to $90 million.

While the absolute level of these efforts may remain small for some time when compared with those of DOD or NASA, the 1971 budget may foretell growth rates for R&D in these areas reminiscent of those in DOD and NASA in 1955–65. A small shift in resources from the major research-sponsoring agencies to other agencies could create a relatively large increase in high priority domestic areas; for example, 3 percent of Defense R&D spending equals 100 percent of the Department of Transportation's R&D costs.

Several complementary factors explain the rise in R&D for social programs. For one thing, the administration has taken the position that much more ought to be known about social problems and their solutions before the government commits itself to massive action and spending. This appears to be the rationale behind the boost in experimental education programs funded by the Office of Education. In other cases, where budgetary constraints have made it impossible sharply to expand broad support programs, the administration is devoting additional R&D efforts to improving knowledge of how increased funds might be most effectively expended when they again become available. In still others, potential technological developments might dramatically multiply the payoff of social investments. This is clearly the hope for Operation Breakthrough, sponsored by HUD (see above, p. 93).

Research and Education

Most basic and biomedical research in the United States is supported by federal grants, particularly those from the National Institutes of Health to universities and research centers. As these funds expanded rapidly during the early 1960s, graduate and professional research and education in American universities became increasingly dependent on them. As the rate of R&D growth has diminished, universities have been compelled both to use more of their own resources and to curtail the expansion of their research and biomedical programs. The federal government now supplies 57 percent of R&D expenditures of colleges and universities, down from 60 percent in 1967. The total amount of R&D money available to universities in 1970 is less in dollar terms (and of course in real terms as well) than it was two years ago. As a result of this drop and the escalation of research costs, colleges and universities will have to produce $200 million more from their own resources in 1970 than they raised in 1967.

Complicating this relationship is the fact that federal R&D funds, channeled primarily through NIH, have become the main instruments for supporting biomedical education in the United States. From the universities' standpoint, scientific research and higher education are a joint enterprise. Accordingly, the cutback in federal R&D has affected not only research but also the basic educational programs of graduate and medical schools.

The leveling off of federal support at a time of rapidly mounting research and educational costs has resulted in serious concern in the academic community. Higher costs have led to a decline in the number of grants; for example, NIH awarded 12,419 research grants in 1965, 10,650 in 1969 and plans 9,867 in 1971. (See Table 4-28.) Younger investigators have been particularly hard hit. The National Science Foundation, often thought of as a "balance wheel," has never received a budget large enough to allow it to play this role effectively.

While the squeeze on R&D expenditures has had a significant impact on higher education, it should be remembered that during the period of exceptional growth in R&D outlays, universities were able to accumulate sizable quantities of research equipment. Outlays for current services may be sustained to some extent by diverting funds from additional capital investment. Whatever the specific impact on

Table 4-28. Number of Grants Made by National Institutes of Health, by Type, Fiscal Years 1969–71

Type of grant	1969 actual	1970 estimate	1971 estimate
Research	10,650	9,762	9,867
Career	195	188	181
Fellowship	4,375	3,081	2,710
Training	4,091	3,870	3,734
Total	19,311	16,901	16,492

Source: *The Budget of the United States Government, Fiscal Year 1971—Appendix*, pp. 400–08.

education of this year's research and development decisions, the more general point remains that program decisions in support of academic research and higher education tend to be separated in budgetary decision making. Since in large measure these activities go together on our nation's campuses, there is a real danger that budgetary decisions independently taken about research and development will have unexpected and perhaps undesirable effects on education.

5. Problems in Some Older Programs

In his budget message, President Nixon focused on the need for "new directions" in federal policies and programs. He described the 1971 budget as "a significantly different set of priorities" from those contained in previous budgets. Yet the President also recognized that this year's budget—like its predecessors—is overwhelmingly a response to choices and commitments made in the past. The President characterized almost 70 percent of the budget as "relatively uncontrollable"; he might have gone on to note that in the nondefense area under the laws currently prevailing, approximately nine of every ten dollars to be spent by the federal government in 1971 will be determined by statutory entitlements and irreversible administrative actions taken in previous years. After a major effort to rearrange priorities in a $200 billion budget, the President was able to devote only $4.6 billion to the expansion of existing programs and the creation of new ones.

In the longer term, changes in the basic statutes authorizing federal programs can significantly affect the budget. This chapter examines, for illustrative purposes, several long-established federal programs and points out some of the ways in which they no longer appear to be serving the public objectives to which they were originally addressed. In one sense the analysis raises nothing new. The problems posed by these programs have long been recognized. But only as the public widely understands the characteristics of such programs will any President be able to secure the support he needs to achieve reforms.

Public Works Projects: Water Resources

Most industrial development is carried out by private industry with private capital. In the case of water resource development, however, much of the investment has traditionally been made by the federal government.

In recent years federal investment in water resource projects has been somewhat more than $1 billion annually. (See Table 5-1.)

Table 5-1. Federal Outlays for Water Resource Development, Various Fiscal Years, 1961–71

Millions of dollars

Type and purpose of outlay	1961	1965	1970	1971
Capital outlays				
Flood control	330	471	432	526
Irrigation and water conservation	109	119	82	91
Navigation	210	266	204	198
Multiple purpose dams with hydropower	363	363	333	435
Operation and maintenance outlays	159	220	312	352
Total	1,171	1,439	1,363	1,602

Source: *The Budget of the United States Government* ... for Fiscal Years 1963, 1967, and 1971.

Operation and maintenance expenditures have been rising gradually with increasing costs and the growing number of projects to be maintained. Water resource investment is planned and carried out by four federal agencies. The Department of Interior's Bureau of Reclamation undertakes projects, primarily in the West, involving a combination of hydroelectric power and irrigation. The Corps of Engineers undertakes flood control, navigation, and hydroelectric power projects on major rivers. The Department of Agriculture is responsible for water resource development on small upstream watersheds. Finally, in the Tennessee Valley, water resource development is carried out by the Tennessee Valley Authority (TVA).

Unlike many other government programs, water resource investment produces an output that has a measurable value—hydroelectric power, damage prevented by flood control, saving in transportation costs from navigation projects on inland waterways, and added crop production on newly irrigated lands. As a consequence, it is possible to estimate a rate of return on such projects, just as it would be for investment by a private firm. Calculations of prospective returns, in the form of benefit-cost analyses, are made for each proposed water resource project and submitted to the Congress as part of the justification for it.

While in theory businesslike calculations are applied to water resource projects, in fact the guidelines used and the political pressure applied in project selection are such that a very large part of the $1 billion-plus annual investment is devoted to projects that yield little if anything in the way of net national benefits.

Two kinds of problems exist. First, the rate of return required of federal water resource projects is very low by almost any reasonable standard. Second, for irrigation, navigation, and flood control projects, the definition of benefits is very questionable, for it encourages the design and acceptance of projects that do not, when realistically evaluated, add to national income or productivity by an amount that justifies their costs.

Rate of Return

Until recently the discount rate, or rate of return used to evaluate federal water resource projects, was set at a level significantly below the current yield on long-term government bonds, and of course far below the 10–15 percent return earned, on the average, by private industrial investment. Investing federal funds in such projects diverts scarce national resources into relatively unproductive uses. During the period from 1946 to 1962, the discount rate used in evaluating federal projects ranged between 2½ and 3 percent. An examination of some 147 Corps of Engineers projects started during those years, at a total cost of $2.6 billion, showed that even on the basis of the dubious definition of benefits used in justifying the projects, two out of five yielded less than a 4½ percent return and three out of five yielded less than 5½ percent.[1] Another examination of six irrigation projects of the Bureau of Reclamation showed that only one yielded a return greater than 5 percent and three showed a loss.

In 1968 the discount rate for evaluating federal water resource projects was adjusted upward to equal the current yield on long-term government bonds. However, the stipulation was made that this rate could be increased by no more than one-quarter of 1 percent in any one year. Currently the applicable rate is 4⅞ percent, still far below the typical yield on private investment and well below the current 6 to 7 percent return on government bonds. Had these latter rates been used in evaluating projects, many of those currently being undertaken would clearly have been rejected.

Navigation Projects

The Corps of Engineers undertakes projects designed to make inland waterways navigable or to improve existing navigable waterways. The benefits from such projects are the savings in transportation costs that inland waterways make possible. In estimating these savings, two questions must be answered: (1) What is the reduction in the cost per ton of traffic carried on the waterway, compared with rail or truck transportation? (2) How many tons of traffic will be carried? Current methods of evaluation tend to overstate both elements of this calculation. For example, the forecasts of future traffic on the waterway make the highly unrealistic assumption that railroads and truck lines will not reduce their rates under competition from the new waterway. The competitive position of the waterway is thereby sharply exaggerated, and the benefits from the project correspondingly overstated.

In 1964 the Corps of Engineers developed new and much more realistic means of estimating the real savings to the nation in transportation costs in place of the previous definition of savings to shippers. It soon became apparent that many potential navigation projects that would have passed the old tests could not be justified under the new criteria. As a consequence, in 1967 the Congress took the unprecedented step of writing into the bill creating the new Department of Transportation a provision that explicitly required the Corps of Engineers to revert to the old, more generous techniques of measuring benefits from navigation projects. Ironically, this language was inserted as a substitute for an administration-sponsored provision that would have given the secretary of transportation responsibility for developing economic criteria for evaluating federal transportation investments.

Once the waterway is built, its services are provided free to barge operators. Fees are not levied even to recover operating and maintenance costs. The taxpayer thus subsidizes not only the capital costs of uneconomic investments, but also project operations. Successive administrations have sought to secure congressional sanctions for modest charges on the use of waterways. None has been successful.

Irrigation

In those parts of the country where water is scarce, federal irrigation projects provide a means of collecting and distributing water for use in growing crops. At the same time, the Department of Agriculture annually spends about $4.5 billion to restrict the production of agricultural output. To a significant extent, therefore, the increase in farm output on newly irrigated land must be matched by a reduction in output in other parts of the country. National income is not increased, but simply transferred from one section of the country to another at a substantial cost to the taxpayer.

The price charged farmers for water from federal irrigation projects is well below its economic cost. Part of the subsidy is paid by the taxpayer, part by consumers of power from hydroelectric facilities whose rates are set high enough to cover some of the subsidy to irrigators. The resulting subsidies, however, do not accrue primarily to farmers who are struggling to make ends meet. They are directed predominantly toward larger farms. One study of federal irrigation projects approved between 1964 and 1967 showed that the value of the water subsidy averaged $122,000 per farm served.[2] This is equivalent to making a gift of $6,700 a year for fifty years to the average farmer concerned. The economic value of the water subsidy to a typical large cotton farm in southern California amounts to about $40,000 a year.[3] In the case of many irrigation projects, therefore, the taxpayer subsidizes high-income farmers through the provision of facilities to add to agricultural output while simultaneously paying the cost of a farm program to reduce farm output.

Flood Control

Federal flood control projects are intended to prevent damage to investments located in flood plains. If the value of damages prevented is greater than the cost of the project, then the project presumably has a favorable benefit-cost ratio and is eligible for federal financing. But in many cases, while damages prevented are indeed greater than project costs, the investments being protected should never have been made on the flood plain in the first place. The economic value of locating there was less than the cost to society of making the investment safe from floods. Moreover, because flood protection is seldom associated with flood plain zoning, the construction of flood protection projects often sharply accelerates investment in the flood plain, including areas of the plain that are only partially protected from floods. As a consequence, it is not uncommon for flood damage to grow after flood protection works have been completed.

Increasingly in recent years, flood protection works have been constructed not to protect existing investments but to make possible future development. The economic consequence, of course, is a large jump in the value of undeveloped land in such areas. The federal taxpayer, who subsidizes the great bulk of the costs for flood protection, is being called upon to lay out ever larger sums primarily for the benefit of land owners and land speculators in the affected areas.

This is not to say that all federal flood protection works are poor investments. But it does imply that a national policy of dealing with flood losses cannot rely solely on such public projects. Flood control policy should encourage rational decisions about the location of private investment in flood plain lands, through flood plain zoning, insurance techniques, and other devices, so that the federal government is not called upon to protect from damage investments that should not have been made in the first place. A requirement that those who benefit from flood protection pay a significant share of the cost of that protection would not only reduce the burden on the federal taxpayer, but would also help to promote sensible investment decisions.

Congressional Appropriations for Public Works

Each year the Congress appropriates funds to start more new public works projects than the President has recommended. Yet each year the Congress reduces the public works appropriations recommended by the President. This sleight of hand is made possible by the way in which public works projects are financed. Such projects take many years to complete. In other parts of the budget—for example, foreign aid—the total estimated cost of a project is appropriated when the project is first started. The funds are then spent as the work progresses. In the case of water resources, however, this "full-funding" approach is not followed. Rather, the Congress each year appropriates the funds necessary to complete that year's work on the project. This means that a very large undertaking can be started with a very small appropriation, since the amount of work done in the first year of a project is usually only a minute fraction of its total cost. The 1971 budget, for example, recommends the start of work on the Tennessee-

Tombigbee Waterway at a total estimated cost of $320 million. But only $1 million will be appropriated in 1971. The 1971 construction budget for the Corps of Engineers amounts to $821 million, but only $16 million of that sum represents appropriations for new starts; the remainder will be required to pay for ongoing work on projects begun in earlier years.

By this means of financing, when the Congress adds new starts to the budget it can increase the total cost of future budgets without raising significantly the appropriations for the immediate year. A new project eventually costing hundreds of millions can be initiated with the immediate consequence of adding only $1 million or $2 million to the current year's appropriations. At the same time a very small proportionate cut in appropriations for ongoing projects—requiring the work to proceed at a slightly slower pace—can more than offset the increase due to the addition of new projects, so that the total appropriation finally enacted is lower than the President's initial request. In subsequent years, of course, as the additional projects get under way and require large annual appropriations, the President is forced to submit budget requests for the much larger sums necessary to complete them.

During the past ten years, administration budgets have recommended 282 new starts on Corps of Engineers construction projects costing an estimated total of $4.1 billion. To these recommendations the Congress added 270 new starts with a total estimated cost of $4.5 billion. But because the first year costs of new starts are typically so small, the Congress had to add only $144 million to administration appropriation requests to get the $4.5 billion of new work under way. To put it differently, by adding only $14 million a year to the public works budget—an amount easily offset by small cuts in ongoing projects—the Congress more than doubled the value of new public works projects recommended by the administration, while on paper it cut the budget each year.

It has often been suggested that public works projects should be put on a full-funding basis, so that the entire cost of a new project would have to be appropriated in the first year. Were this approach to be adopted, the addition of new projects to the President's budget would result in full disclosure—that is, the full cost of the additional projects would show up as an increase in the total appropriations for the year. Precisely for this reason, the Congress has always resisted the full-funding approach to public works. This is well illustrated by the following exchange, taken from a Senate hearing some years ago on appropriations dealing with full funding:

GENERAL ITSCHNER [Corps of Engineers]. What I am proposing is: For construction projects we would come to you just once for a single appropriation.

If we needed more money later, if we could not do the job for the amount that we originally said we would require, then we would have to come before you to explain why, and obtain an additional appropriation.

But we would still appear before you every year anyway, both for the new starts and for operation and maintenance and any other expenses.

SENATOR X: Are you suggesting that a lump sum appropriation for a project such as John Day Dam, that cost how much?

GENERAL ITSCHNER: $418 million or something like that.

SENATOR X: Talk about shouting pork barrel, you would really get it there I guess. That would make the initiation of a large project almost impossible.

GENERAL ITSCHNER: This is just a suggestion. I recognize that disadvantage.

SENATOR X: We would consider it a disadvantage.

GENERAL ITSCHNER: There are many disadvantages to it, but in the end I think it would save money. I recognize there are problems in doing it. But after the first year or two, after the system was put into effect, the overall bill should be no greater than it is now.

SENATOR X: I understand that, but without having studied the matter too deeply, I feel that the public reaction to a request for say a tenth or a fifth of the total cost of a project is bad enough, without going into this.

The first thing opponents of resource development would say is, "Look at the money that is being appropriated over the budget this year" when as a matter of fact, under the present system, if you were to provide funds to start the John Day Dam which would probably take six or seven years to build, you would provide only that amount of money required for the first year.

SENATOR Y: If we asked for the total amount we wouldn't get it.

SENATOR X: That is the point. I believe that it would be much more difficult to obtain the funds for new starts under that system than under the present method.

Impacted Aid

"Impacted aid" is the program under which the federal government provides assistance to school districts that have a significant number of students whose parents are federal employees. The program originated during the Korean war, when school districts in which federal military installations were located were confronted with rapidly rising school enrollments and costs.[4] The law makes eligible for impacted aid any school district that has at least 3 percent, or 300, federally connected pupils. "Federally connected" means either that a parent works *and* lives on federal property (so-called "a" children) or that a parent works *or* lives on federal property ("b" children). Note that in order to receive assistance, the district need not be the site of the federal installation. Each eligible district calculates its federal "entitlement" by multiplying the sum of its "a" children and one-half of its "b" children by the largest of the following:

• the locally raised revenue per pupil in comparable districts in the same state;

• the per pupil local revenue in the same "grouping" of districts in the state;

• one-half the state average of total per pupil cost; or

• one-half the national average of total per pupil cost.

If the Congress appropriates less than the full entitlement, assistance to each school district is scaled down proportionately. In 1969 and 1970, obligations were $506 million for aid to the operating budgets of eligible districts.

Anomalies in the Way the Formula Works

1. *The amount of assistance is often unrelated to the presence of nontaxable federal property.* In the case in which parents live on private taxable property in school district X but work on federal property in district Y, district X is the recipient of the aid. The most extreme example is provided by Montgomery County, Maryland, a very wealthy bedroom suburb of Washington, D.C., which receives substantial impacted aid in payment for the "burden" imposed on its schools by children whose parents work in Washington. If there is any loss of property tax, however, it is in Washington—not in Montgomery County. This situation is unique, but in 1969 Montgomery County received almost $6 million in impacted school aid—more than was received by the District of Columbia.

2. *Most of the districts aided are not heavily burdened by federal installations.* In 56 percent of the school districts aided, less than 6 percent of the students are federally connected. Heavily impacted areas—those with federally connected enrollments of 25 percent or

more—compose only 9 percent of the school districts aided. The first group of schools gets 28 percent of the money; the second gets 25 percent.

3. *Students who impose the greatest burden account for a small part of all eligible students.* Students whose parents both live and work on federal property account for less than 14 percent of federally connected students. Those whose parents live on private taxable property account for 86 percent of all eligible students in districts receiving impacted aid. Moreover, the largest single category of federally connected students (35 percent) are those who live on private property in school district X but whose parents work on federal property in school district Y.

4. *The impacted aid program distorts efforts by states to equalize educational opportunities.* Many states give relatively large school aid payments to school districts that have low property assessments per pupil. Under existing federal law, a state may not take impacted aid into account in its formula for school aid equalization, and state equalization aid does not affect federal payments. The result is that school districts in which many federal installations are located (and which thus have low property values per student) receive both impacted aid from the federal government *and* equalization payments from the state for essentially the same burden. Some states (New Mexico, for example) have avoided this problem by not adopting equalization formulas; others have been thwarted in their equalization attempts.

5. *The formula sometimes makes school districts eligible without any real change in their circumstances.* Consider a medium-sized school district that spends relatively little on each student. Of its 10,000 pupils, 299 have parents who work in a government-owned, contractor-operated plant, but live in private homes ("b" children). The school district spends $300 per pupil—$10 raised from local residential taxes, $50 from taxing the inventories of the government-owned plant, and the rest from the state—for a total of $3 million. This school district is not eligible for impacted aid because less than 3 percent of its pupils are federally connected. Now, the U.S. post office (which does not count as federal property under the act) assigns one employee to sort mail in the government-owned plant. The postal employee has one child, already in the local schools. At this point, the school district becomes eligible for impacted aid, for it now has 300

"b" children out of 10,000 students. Under the law, the school district is entitled to 150 (since "b" children count as half) times $300 (half the national per pupil cost—a method chosen for illustrative purposes), or $45,000. Thus the school district, whose objective circumstances are unaltered, receives a bonus of 1½ percent of its school budget from the federal government. It could lower local property taxes by almost half (impacted aid is $4.50 per student out of $10 per student in local property sources), or spend the proceeds on school enrichment. While overdrawn, this example illustrates the possibility of overpayment under the impacted aid program.

Recent Congressional Proposals

The Ninety-first Congress is considering legislation to make children who reside in public housing eligible for impacted aid. A leading motive of proponents of this change is to help the cities. Although public housing by law is not taxable property, local housing authorities do make payments in lieu of taxes to municipalities and school districts. To the extent that public housing reduces the taxing ability of the school district, the rate of payment under impacted aid would probably be at least double the real burden. Moreover, it has not been demonstrated that public housing increases the number of pupils in a school district. This change in the law would add $250 million in entitlements and thereby create pressures for high appropriations in the future.

Cities would benefit unevenly from this amendment because the amount of public housing varies significantly from city to city. For every $1 per student (counting all students in the schools) received by the Los Angeles school district, the Boston school district would receive $11. For every $1 of aid for a low-income child (whether or not publicly housed) in Detroit, $16 would be paid for a low-income child in Nashville.

The Administration's Proposals

The fiscal 1971 legislative program of the administration includes amendments to the impacted aid law that would have the following effects:

1. When a parent works on federal property located in the same district as his child's school, the child will "count" as 40 percent in

calculating the district's entitlement (compared with 50 percent at present).

2. When a parent works on federal property in a district other than that in which his child attends school, the child will count as only 20 percent (compared with 50 percent at present).

3. Although a district will continue to be eligible if 3 percent of its pupils are federally connected, it will be entitled to aid only for those in excess of 3 percent.

4. In place of the present alternative methods of computing per capita entitlement, the administration proposes a fixed rate of 60 percent of the national average expenditure per pupil for all districts.

If these amendments are approved by the Congress, they will go a long way toward remedying the anomalies described above.

Farm Price Supports: Who Gets the Benefits?

An earlier section of this review discusses the various choices that the administration and the Congress must face this year in extending the farm subsidy program. In the past, much of the public support for farm price subsidies has stemmed from the knowledge that, on the average, farm families had much lower incomes than other families: in 1968, the median net income of a farm family was $5,800 compared with $8,800 for nonfarm families. Farm price supports have been seen by many as a relatively expensive, often inefficient, but nevertheless necessary device to narrow the gap in living standards between rural and urban citizens. In recent years, however, data have become available that make it possible to estimate, albeit roughly, which groups receive the major benefits from price support programs. In summary, the data indicate that the great bulk of the subsidies go to farmers whose incomes exceed the nonfarm average, while only a small portion finds it way to the low-income families whose need for improved living standards was the basic justification for the program.

The farm programs are exceedingly complex, but their elements can be simply summarized: (1) The farm programs pay direct cash subsidies to producers of major crops; (2) in return, farmers agree to restrict their planting of crops, thereby reducing supply, raising prices, and further augmenting farm income. The first element of subsidy comes directly from the budget and is financed by the tax-payer. The second element, through supply restrictions, provides farmers with higher incomes in the marketplace and is paid by consumers in the form of higher prices.

Both kinds of benefits—direct cash subsidies and higher prices in the marketplace—are distributed among farmers roughly in proportion to their output of farm products. Direct cash payments are based on acreage allotments; the larger the farm, the larger the payments. Higher prices obviously benefit farmers in proportion to their output. In 1968, about 500,000 large farms with annual sales in excess of $20,000—but accounting for only 17 percent of all farms—produced almost 70 percent of farm output; consequently, they received most of the direct and indirect benefits of the farm subsidy programs. At the other end of the scale were 1.6 million small farms with annual sales of $5,000 or less. They represented more than 50 percent of all farms, but they produced only 6 percent of total farm output and received a correspondingly small share of subsidy benefits.

In 1968 direct cash subsidies amounted to $3.5 billion. The value of the indirect price support subsidy is difficult to estimate, since it represents the difference between what farmers actually receive in the marketplace and what they would have received in the absence of price supports. Although a precise calculation of this difference is impossible, a number of agricultural economists, including those in the Department of Agriculture, have made rough estimates of the gap. Their estimates indicate that, in the absence of farm price supports, farm income earned in the marketplace would be $3 billion to $4 billion lower than its current level. Therefore, the total benefits from farm subsidy programs amount to about $7 billion, half from cash subsidy payments and half from price supports in the market.

Using data on the production of farm commodities by farms of various sizes and other information on the distribution of direct cash payments, it is possible to make rough estimates of how that $7 billion is distributed among farm income groups of various sizes.

The 17 percent of American farms with sales of more than $20,000 have an average net income of $19,000 a year. They receive about 60 percent of the $7 billion in total benefits from the farm program, or an average of $8,000 per farm. At the other extreme, the 1.6 million small farms, with farm sales of $5,000 or less, had average incomes from farming of $1,300. (A very large number of these farmers also had income from nonfarm sources; indeed, for the group as a whole, average income from nonfarm sources was $5,900, for a total of

$7,100.) While these farmers constituted more than 50 percent of the farm population, they received only 11 percent of the total benefits from farm subsidy programs. Their incomes were raised, on the average, by only $400 through the subsidies.

Studies of the distribution of subsidy benefits for individual crops tell essentially the same story. The top fifth of sugar cane growers, ranked by size of acreage, receives more than 80 percent of farm subsidy payments, while the smallest one-fifth receives only 1 percent; the top fifth of cotton growers receives 70 percent of the benefits and the smallest fifth only 2 percent. In the case of feed grains, the payments are more evenly distributed, but even here, the largest fifth of producers receives 56 percent and the smallest fifth only 1 percent of the benefits.

Some farms receive extraordinarily large cash subsidies. In 1967 five farms received more than $1 million each, fifteen received payments ranging between $500,000 and $1 million, 388 farms received checks ranging from $100,000 to $500,000, and 1,285 were paid between $50,000 and $100,000. In the state of Mississippi, for example, 817 large farms received $38.3 million in direct federal farm subsidies. Federal payments to the state for aid to dependent children totaled only $10 million. The average federal payment to the large farms was $47,000 each; the average federal payment per dependent child was $80.

While it is undeniably true that average farm income is significantly lower than nonfarm income, the farm price support program has not served primarily to redistribute income in favor of poor farmers. Those who receive most of its benefits already have net incomes substantially above the average received by the nonfarm population.

Maritime Subsidies

The federal government directly and indirectly subsidizes the American merchant marine by about $650 million to $750 million a year. The subsidy program supports both an active U.S. merchant fleet and U.S. shipyards. The operating costs of about 300 U.S. flag ships carrying "liner" cargo—that is, manufactured goods of all kinds—and crewed by U.S. citizens are subsidized to keep their costs in line with those of foreign competitors. Operators of subsidized ships must buy them from U.S. shipyards, where prices are more than double those in foreign yards; the government pays the difference. Under "cargo preference" laws, all military cargoes and 50 percent of Agency for International Development shipments and subsidized food exports under Public Law 480 must be carried on U.S. flag ships—at well above foreign rates. Other forms of subsidy include free medical care for U.S. merchant seamen and certain tax advantages for U.S. shipowners. In addition to making these budgetary outlays, the federal government requires that all coastal and "offshore" shipments (for example, from New York to Galveston or San Francisco to Hawaii) be carried on U.S. flag ships. As a consequence, shippers incur costs substantially higher than what they would pay to foreign carriers. The amount of this indirect subsidy totals $100 million to $150 million a year.

National defense considerations provide the principal justification for the subsidy program. The operating subsidies and cargo preference laws sustain a fleet of U.S. flag ships to be available in time of war to carry essential cargoes. The shipbuilding subsidies presumably maintain shipyard capacity that might be needed in wartime.

Substantial questions can be raised about the real benefits to national security resulting from a subsidized merchant marine:

1. The operating and cargo preference subsidies keep some 400 U.S. flag ships engaged in foreign trade. But there are also 440 unsubsidized ships owned by U.S. firms operating under flags of convenience (primarily of Panama, Honduras, and Liberia) that are contractually committed to serve the United States in time of emergency. In addition there are the merchant fleets of our NATO allies, totaling 7,600 ships. While national security considerations do affirm the need for a U.S. flag fleet in case of war, that requirement needs to be put in the context of these other shipping assets.

2. Ironically, unless the President declares a national emergency, it turns out to be very difficult for the Defense Department to gain access to subsidized ships in limited war situations. During the early days of the Vietnam war, U.S. flag operators—subsidized all these years for national defense purposes—were most reluctant to give up their commercial business and carry defense cargo to Vietnam. Indeed, more foreign flag operators offered ships to the Defense Department than did U.S. operators.

3. Primarily because of naval work, the American shipbuilding industry is the largest in the world. However, of 110,000 production

workers, only 7,500 are normally employed in building subsidized merchant vessels. To pay $350 million to $400 million a year in ship-building subsidies (as would be the case under the proposed new maritime program) in order to add this small amount to U.S. ship-building capability is to pay a high price indeed. Moreover, we learned in the Second World War that shipbuilding capacity could be expanded very rapidly. (Between 1939 and 1943, U.S. shipbuilding capacity expanded fourteenfold.)

4. To the extent that it is desirable to increase the number of U.S. flag ships in operation, allowing U.S. shipowners to buy ships abroad would seem to make much sense. So long as shipowners are required to buy their ships in the United States, the number they can purchase will be limited sharply by the very high subsidy the federal budget must carry for each ship built.

Large maritime subsidies are sometimes justified as a means of injecting a competitive U.S. merchant marine into the world shipping market, thereby protecting U.S. shippers from high cargo rates set by foreign shipping cartels. In fact, the potential competitive influence of U.S. ships on world cargo rates is substantially defeated by the way the subsidy program is run. Protected preference cargoes make up a large part of the export value of goods carried by the subsidized fleet, leaving only part of its capacity to exert an influence in the competitive market. The subsidy is so structured as to discourage competitive efficiency and limit the freedom of subsidized operators: indeed, U.S. lines are a high-cost, not a low-cost element of the world's shipping fleet. Potential competition is further reduced by the payment of subsidies for voyages on predetermined and narrowly defined trade routes that restrict the competitive movement of vessels from one route to another. Finally, measures to improve the competitiveness of the U.S. merchant fleet are affected by union manning rules that often obstruct the adoption of new technology.

The Congress has before it an administration proposal to revise the current maritime subsidy program substantially. The program has two major aspects:

Reform. The operating subsidy would be restructured to be less a pure "cost-plus" subsidy and to provide greater incentives for efficiency. The ship construction subsidy would be changed to encourage mass production techniques, and the legislation would allow a gradual lowering of the subsidized differential between the costs of U.S. and foreign ships.

Expansion. The current rate of ship construction would be trebled to about thirty new ships a year. Tramp ships carrying bulk cargo would be made eligible for operating subsidies. The administration estimates that the expanded construction program would add about $100 million a year in new costs. However, unless the move to lower the U.S.-foreign differential is successful, the added construction costs could be much larger.

In considering future policy, it is useful to view the maritime program in its principal parts—the subsidies to the merchant fleet and subsidies to U.S. shipyards. With respect to the first, a change in the subsidy structure to encourage efficiency, to reduce or eliminate cargo preferences on nonmilitary shipments, and to provide the Defense Department with reliable access to U.S. ships in time of emergency could promote a merchant marine that would be both more efficient and of greater service to national security. Regarding the second, one may ask whether the requirement that all U.S. flag ships be built in U.S. shipyards will significantly increase national security. To enlarge the construction subsidy program is a costly means of expanding the merchant fleet that would add little or nothing to national preparedness. On the other hand, to allow U.S. ship owners to buy some or all of their vessels abroad would increase the effectiveness of the merchant marine and put competitive pressure on U.S. shipyards.

6. Long-Term Projections

THIS YEAR, FOR THE FIRST TIME, both the budget and the Economic Report of the President provide long-term projections of the overall economy and the federal budget. As the budget message puts it:

The President's ability to control budget decisions is limited by the long-range impact of past decisions as to the nature and dimensions of resource allocation. Budget control can be improved by projecting available resources and potential claims on them. Such projections require assumptions about the future course of economic, legislative, international, and other events and are necessarily rough and arbitrary. Nevertheless, they should be undertaken to present a tentative indication of our future fiscal environment.

The projections do not attempt to forecast the future course of the total budget. Rather they seek to answer the following questions: (1) Under current tax laws, by how much will federal revenues grow as the economy advances over the next several years? (2) Given current federal spending programs and those proposed by the President in the 1971 budget, by how much will federal spending rise over the same period because of increases in prices, wages, workloads, and the fruition of currently proposed programs?

The difference between the two projected totals—expected revenues and committed or proposed expenditures—is the "fiscal dividend." It is an estimate of the resources available to the federal government to support new programs, to expand existing ones, to cut taxes, or to retire debt. The projection does not indicate how the fiscal dividend might be used, but simply estimates its magnitude.

178

This chapter gives the results of an independent fiscal projection of revenues and expenditures for 1973 and 1975. The projected fiscal dividend for 1975 is very similar to that shown in the 1971 budget. (The budget does not present a 1973 estimate.) The projections in this chapter are presented in greater detail, however, and several alternative outcomes are shown. In 1967 the President's Commission on Budget Concepts, whose chairman is now secretary of the treasury and whose staff director is the current budget director, recommended that independent research organizations undertake five-year projections of revenues and of expenditure changes flowing from current and proposed decisions. The commission also recommended that the projections show alternative outcomes related to varying assumptions. The estimates in this chapter attempt to be responsive to that recommendation.

Basic Economic Assumptions

The pattern of real output growth between now and 1975 assumed in these projections is almost identical with the estimates presented by the Council of Economic Advisers in its 1970 report. *Potential* gross national product (GNP)—the output that the economy is capable of producing at high employment levels—is assumed to rise 4.3 percent a year from the latter part of 1969 to 1975. *Actual* GNP— the output that is produced each year—is projected to increase very little in 1970 (slightly more than 1 percent in constant dollars). A gap opens between actual and potential GNP, and the unemployment rate for the year as a whole rises from the 3.5 percent of 1969 to 4.4 percent. Beginning in late 1970, output begins to rise parallel to the economy's potential, but still remains below it. By 1973 the gap is assumed to close, and the unemployment rate drops to 3.8 percent. (See Table 6-1.) From then to 1975, actual and potential GNP are identical.

A fairly marked deceleration in price increases over the period can be inferred from a comparison of the Budget Bureau projections of current-dollar GNP in 1975 with the constant-dollar projections of the Council. The rate of price increase assumed in the budget projections appears to taper off from 4¼ percent in 1970 to about 1¾ percent by 1973 and then to remain at that level. In the projection here the annual rate of price increase also tapers off, but only to 2¼ per-

Table 6-1. Basic Economic Assumptions Underlying Projections, Fiscal Years 1969, 1973, and 1975

Dollar amounts in billions

Economic indicator	1969 actual	1973 projected	1975 projected
GNP, current dollars	932.1	1,250	1,428
GNP, 1969 dollars	932.1	1,100	1,195
Price deflator, 1969=100	100.0	113.7	119.5
Unemployment rate, percent	3.5	3.8	3.8
Personal income, excluding transfers	681.7	910	1,035
Corporate profits before taxes	93.8	132	152

Source: For 1969, *Economic Indicators*, March 1970; for 1973 and 1975, authors' estimates.

cent. This seems to be more consistent with the 3.8 percent unemployment rate used in the projections. However, projections of the fiscal dividend using both sets of price assumptions have been calculated and will be shown later in the chapter.

Revenues

Given the assumptions about economic growth, including an estimate of personal income and corporate profits, federal revenues under existing tax laws have been calculated. Because major changes in federal tax rates have been so frequent in recent years (the tax cuts of 1964 and 1965, the surcharge in 1968, the tax reform of 1969), estimates of the relationship between tax revenues and income are necessarily subject to more than the usual error. Possibly because of these statistical difficulties, the projections of revenues for 1975, shown in Table 6-2, are higher than those presented in the budget message, even after an adjustment is made for the lower price increases assumed in the budget projections.

Several major assumptions underlie the estimates of revenues shown in Table 6-2.

1. The increase in social security payroll tax rates scheduled under current law will go into effect. Similarly, it was assumed that the maximum taxable wage base under the social security program would be increased from the present $7,800 to $9,000 on January 1, 1971, as proposed by the President. The scheduled increases in tax rates and wage base add $12 billion to revenues by 1975.

2. The increase in unemployment insurance taxes and in the wage base will take place as proposed by the President.

**Table 6-2. Projections of Federal Revenues by Category,
and Comparison of Various Projections of Total Revenue,
Fiscal Years 1971, 1973, and 1975**

Billions of dollars

Revenue category	1971	1973	1975
Revenues, before allowing for the 1969 tax reform:			
Individual income taxes	93.8	113.0	134.0
Corporation income taxes	32.1	44.0	51.0
Social insurance taxes and contributions	49.1	61.5	68.8
Excise taxes	17.5	17.8	17.4
Estate and gift taxes	3.6	4.1	4.5
Customs duties	2.3	2.8	3.3
Miscellaneous receipts	3.6	4.3	4.9
Subtotal	201.9	247.5	284.0
Less: Net revenue cost of 1969 tax reform[a]	*+0.2*	*−6.5*	*−8.0*
Total revenue	202.1	241.0	276.0

Comparison of various projections of total revenue

Basis or source	1971	1973	1975
Projection presented above	202.1	241	276
Projection based on budget document price assumptions	202.1	240	272
Projection presented in budget document	202.1	n.e.	266

Source: Authors' estimates and *The Budget of the United States Government, Fiscal Year 1971*. Details may not add to totals because of rounding.

n.e. = not estimated.

a. The cost of the tax reform is a net figure resulting from an *increase* in revenues as a consequence of repeal of the investment credit and various other tax increases (+$7.5 billion by 1975), which is more than offset by a *decrease* in revenues from the tax relief provisions (−$15.5 billion by 1975).

3. A gradual phasing out of excise taxes on automobiles and telephone service will occur as scheduled under present law.

On these assumptions, federal revenues, before taking into account the revenue implications of the 1969 tax reform, would rise from $202 billion in fiscal 1971 to $247 billion in 1973 and to $284 billion in 1975. However, the tax reform act will reduce revenues by $6 billion in 1973 and $8 billion in 1975. Total revenues therefore will rise to $241 billion by 1973 and $276 billion by 1975.

Federal revenues in 1973 and 1975 will account for a slightly smaller proportion of GNP than they did in 1970. This decrease is due to the expiration of the surcharge and to the relief provisions of the reform law. Once these reductions are taken into account, however, federal revenues maintain a roughly constant ratio of 20 percent of GNP in each of the projection years. Under current tax laws, therefore, including the President's proposed changes in payroll taxes, about one-fifth of the nation's economic growth will automatically be made available through the tax system for increased federal activities.

Expenditures

The expenditure projection is made up of several elements:

1. The "automatic" increase in spending under existing federal programs stemming from rising workloads and growing numbers of people statutorily entitled to benefits. Included in this category are such factors as the growth in the number of social security beneficiaries; rising caseloads in the public assistance programs; growing numbers of retired military and civilian employees of the federal government; returning veterans from Vietnam eligible for readjustment benefits; an increase in visitors to national parks; the growth in meat and poultry inspection; and so forth.

2. The pay increases that the federal government must grant simply to keep federal pay comparable with that in private industry. Even if the Congress postpones this year's federal pay increase for six months, as requested by the President, the increases will occur eventually.

3. The impact of rising prices on federal program costs. Under some programs, such as Medicare and Medicaid, higher costs automatically result in higher expenditures, since the bills must be paid. But in other cases—for example, federal grants for elementary and secondary education or for research and development—nothing requires the Congress or the administration to increase grant outlays to match rising costs. Nevertheless, the projections allow for increases in these programs to match the rise in costs. In other words, the projections show the dollar cost, in 1973 and 1975, of maintaining the *real* purchasing power of such programs at today's level, though in many cases there is no statutory requirement to do so. This seems a realistic approach that is more or less matched by actual practice. In the 1971 budget, for example, no major expansion is proposed in grants under Title I of the Elementary and Secondary Education Act. Nonetheless, appropriations increases are requested that are roughly sufficient to offset rising costs and prices.

4. The future costs of currently proposed new programs or program expansion. Many of the initiatives proposed in the budget for 1971 cost little in that year, but are planned to expand significantly in the

future. Revenue sharing, urban mass transit grants, and the family assistance program are cases in point. In other situations, expenditures lag far behind program activity; commitments to states during 1971 for grant assistance in the construction of waste treatment facilities, for example, will not show up as expenditures until the facilities are being built in 1972, 1973, or even later years. The projections allow for this phenomenon.

5. Financial adjustments to the budget. The 1971 budget plans several financial transactions that reduce expenditures solely in that year. The proposed sale of the Alaska Railroad and the transfer of $800 million from the oil escrow account are examples. Future budgets will be higher in the absence of these negative offsets. Similarly, the very large sales of financial assets planned for 1971 probably cannot be sustained at that level in future years. This will also cause an upward adjustment in later budgets.

Table 6-3 summarizes the expenditure projections for 1973 and 1975. The central projection assumes the military budget at the pre-Vietnam baseline figure developed in Chapter 2 (Vietnam outlays tapering off to $1.5 billion in fiscal 1973 and $1 billion in 1975; total

Table 6-3. Projections of Changes in Federal Expenditures by Cause, Fiscal Years 1971–73 and 1973–75; and Comparison of Various Projections of Total Expenditures, Fiscal Years 1971, 1973, and 1975

Billions of dollars

Cause of change	1971–73	1973–75
Pay increases	5.0	3.5
Price increases	10.0	10.0
Major workloads	10.0	9.0
New or expanded programs	7.5	3.5
Financial adjustment	3.5	0.0
Reductions in military budget (in 1971 dollars)	−8.5	−0.5
Reductions in other programs	−1.0	0.0
Net changes	+26.5	+25.5

Comparison of various projections of total expenditures			
Basis or source	1971	1973	1975
Projection reflecting changes itemized above	200.8	227	253
Projection based on budget document price assumptions	200.8	226	250
Projection presented in budget document	200.8	n.e.	244

Source: Same as Table 6-2.
n.e. = not estimated.

Table 6-4. Projected Increases in Expenditures, Selected Programs, Fiscal Years 1971–73 and 1973–75

Billions of dollars

Program	1971–73	1973–75
Social security (OASDI)	6.7	5.3
Medicare and Medicaid	3.2	3.7
Military and civilian retirement	1.7	2.3
Public assistance[a]	1.0	1.2
Family assistance plan[a]	3.0	0.5
Highways	0.9	0.9
Housing	0.7	1.0
Revenue sharing	1.9	2.3
Urban mass transit	0.3	0.3
Military and civilian pay	5.0	3.5

Source: Authors' estimates.

a. Public assistance outlays are projected on the basis of current programs. The projection for the family assistance program is a *net* figure, that is, the difference between the total costs of the new program and what the costs would have been under the current public assistance law.

defense spending of $72 billion in 1971, $70 billion in 1973, and $75 billion in 1975). This defense budget implies a reduction in *real* expenditures of about $9 billion, more than offset by the impact of rising prices and wages and by increased military retirement costs.

Projections for some of the more important individual programs are shown in Table 6-4. In each case, of course, the validity of the projection depends on the specific assumptions with respect to the increase in workloads, prices, and wages.

Social security. The projection assumes a continued increase in the number of aged beneficiaries and an increase in benefit levels in line with rises in the cost of living. The President's proposed increases in the social security program, as spelled out in the budget message, are also incorporated.

Medicare and Medicaid. Continued increases in beneficiaries and in the rate at which beneficiaries utilize the program are projected. In addition, hospital costs and doctor fees are projected to continue rising at a more rapid rate than the general price index, but this gap will narrow somewhat as general inflation subsides in the later years of the projection.

Military and civilian retired pay. Given the age structure of both the federal civilian work force and the regular armed forces, large increases will occur in the number of persons receiving retirement benefits. In both cases current law calls for automatic cost-of-living adjustments plus an extra 1 percent improvement for each 3 percent rise in prices.

Public assistance. Aid to Families with Dependent Children is the major component of this expenditure item. In both 1967 and 1968 the number of recipients under this program increased by 14 percent, and by late 1969 the annual increase had risen to 18 percent. The projection assumes that if the basic program were unchanged, the number of recipients would continue to rise, but at lower rates than in the past few years, tapering off from a 10 percent growth rate in 1972 to 6 percent in 1975. The projection also assumes that average benefit payments would be increased in line with rises in the cost of living plus some small additional improvements.

Family assistance plan. The costs of this program and associated welfare reforms are *net* costs. That is, they represent the difference between what the new plan will cost and what a continuation of existing public assistance programs would cost. In 1971 the budget projects a net cost of only $500 million, since the new plan is scheduled to take effect late in the year. The first full-year net cost is estimated at $4.4 billion. These projections assume that there will be some increases in the level of benefits between now and 1975. Specifically they assume that the minimum level of benefits for a family of four, which the proposed legislation sets at $1,600, will be increased to $2,000 in 1973 and to $2,400 in 1975; that benefit levels for other family sizes will be scaled up proportionately; and that state and local governments will increase the supplementary benefits they pay, over and above the family assistance plan, by an average of about 5 percent a year. However, since the income of eligible beneficiaries from wages and other sources is also expected to rise, the number of low-income persons eligible for the new benefits will decline, as will the income gap to be made up for those remaining eligible. Moreover, the costs of the existing public assistance program would probably have risen quite rapidly, as explained above. As a consequence, the *net* costs of the family assistance plan—after a sharp jump in 1972, the first full year of operation—are not projected to rise significantly in future years, even though benefit levels are assumed to increase.

Highways. Highway expenditures are projected to rise to the level of trust fund revenues. In 1974 or 1975 the current program will expire. However, the projection assumes that the gasoline and other trust fund taxes will be retained and that some combination of highway and other transportation expenditures will be made at a rate no less than that permitted by the yield from these taxes.

Housing. The 1971 budget calls for commitments to be made for the construction or rehabilitation of almost 600,000 subsidized housing units for low- and moderate-income families. Even a simple continuation of this rate, without any increase, will add steadily to the stock of housing units on which the government is paying subsidy. Although rising incomes among subsidized tenants or owners will gradually reduce the average subsidy per housing unit, the total cost will still increase.

Urban mass transit and revenue sharing. These projections simply reflect official administration figures made available when the programs were announced.

The Fiscal Dividend

Table 6-5 combines the revenue and the expenditure projections and shows the fiscal dividend. It provides an estimate of the sums that are likely to become available for use in one, or some combination, of four ways: (1) to expand existing programs; (2) to undertake new public programs; (3) to run a budget surplus for purposes of economic stability, lower interest rates, and a relatively buoyant housing market; and (4) to cut taxes.

If revenues are estimated without taking account of the tax reform law, the potential surplus in the budget would be $20.5 billion in 1973 and $31 billion in 1975. This surplus would have been available for

Table 6-5. The Fiscal Dividend, Alternative 1, Fiscal Years 1973 and 1975

Billions of dollars

Conditions defining Alternative 1	1973	1975
Revenues, before allowing for the 1969 tax reform	247½	284
Expenditures	227	253
Fiscal dividend, before allowing for tax reform	20½	31
Less: Revenue loss from tax reform	6½	8
Fiscal dividend after allowing for tax reform	14	23
Less: Budget surplus at high employment levels, probably needed to		
achieve housing goals while avoiding inflation	8	10
Fiscal dividend, Alternative 1	**6**	**13**

Source: Authors' estimates.

the four uses described above. Some $6.5 billion and $8 billion, in 1973 and 1975, respectively, have been dedicated to tax cuts by the tax reform act. This leaves a dividend of $14 billion in 1973 and $23 billion in 1975.

In fiscal 1971 the high employment surplus is in the neighborhood of $7 billion to $8 billion. This is the surplus that would be yielded by existing tax rates were the economy to operate in calendar 1970 at its full potential, with unemployment at 3.8 percent. It is difficult to see how the housing goals set by the administration can be achieved in the absence of a high employment surplus at least equal to that of 1970 as a percentage of GNP. The housing goals call for an increase in residential construction from 3.5 percent of GNP in 1969 to 4.1 percent in 1975. If this is to happen, some other components of GNP must fall in percentage terms. Yet with transfer payments rising sharply and with the bulk of tax relief in the reform act going to individuals rather than to business firms, consumption expenditures as a percent of GNP are unlikely to fall and indeed should probably rise. The repeal of the investment credit may lead to a decline in the share of GNP devoted to business investment, but it is most unlikely to decline by more than the combined rise in residential construction and consumption expenditures. In these circumstances, failure to achieve a budget surplus in the range currently prevailing would probably lead to high interest rates, credit scarcity, and failure to reach the housing goals.

It would, of course, be possible to support housing construction through direct federal loans to homeowners, partially negating the need for the budget surplus. But this would obviously not increase the fiscal dividend usable for other programs. It would simply shift some of the surplus to budget outlays on direct loans.

It would also be possible to reduce the housing goals. Decent housing standards are an important objective, but when priority judgments have to be made there is no reason to consider them immutable. If fewer houses were built than the present goals contemplate, it would be possible to increase other budget expenditures, to budget for a smaller surplus and a tighter monetary policy, and to accept higher interest rates. Whether this should be done depends on national judgments of the relative importance of housing as against other areas such as pollution control, education, or urban mass transit.

Assuming that the housing goals are pursued and allowing for a conservative estimate of the necessary budget surplus (or for a similar amount of direct federal mortgage support), the net fiscal dividend would appear to be in the neighborhood of $6 billion for 1973 and $13 billion for 1975. The fiscal dividend, it will be recalled, assumes that Vietnam expenditures fall to $1.5 billion in 1973 and $1 billion in 1975. Should Vietnam expenditures be higher than assumed here, and given the assumption with respect to the rest of the defense budget, then of course the fiscal dividend would be correspondingly reduced.

Alternative Policies To Change the Fiscal Dividend

The size of the fiscal dividend shown for 1975 in Table 6-5 is about the same as that which results from the projections of the Council of Economic Advisers and the Budget Bureau, when the latter's estimates are adjusted to reflect the budget surplus needed to accommodate the housing goals. In all of these calculations, the amount available in 1973 and 1975 is exceedingly small compared to the aspirations of various parts of the nation for expanded federal programs to control pollution, to alleviate the financial problems in higher education, to deal with mounting crime rates, to improve the educational, health, and job opportunities of the poor, and to help states and particularly large central cities to overcome serious financial problems.

The fiscal dividend projected in these calculations is not unchangeable, however. It reflects the future consequences of current tax and expenditure policies, which can be changed either to enlarge or to decrease the fiscal dividend. Two sets of illustrative alternatives are shown in Table 6-6. They draw mainly on the discussions of policy alternatives in Chapters 2 and 4.

The potential fiscal dividends shown in the table vary widely, depending on decisions about military spending, taxes, and farm programs. They range from about $36 billion to a negative dividend of $5 billion (which means that to achieve the assumed levels of defense and farm price support spending, other programs would have to be cut). Although there is nothing sacrosanct about these particular alternatives, large changes in the potential sums available for domestic programs can realistically come from only two places: changes in defense spending and changes in tax rates. Program reforms and elimination of outmoded federal activities are obvious means of enlarging

Table 6-6. The Fiscal Dividend, Alternatives 2 and 3, Fiscal Year 1975[a]
Billions of dollars

Conditions defining alternatives		1975
Fiscal dividend, Alternative 1 (from Table 6–5)		**13**
Alternative 2:		
Reduce military expenditures to the lowest of the options shown in Table 2-5 (from $75 billion to $58 billion)	17	
Adopt the low set of options on farm policy shown in Table 4-15	2	
Continue automobile and telephone excise taxes at current rates, rather than allowing scheduled reduction	4	
Fiscal dividend, Alternative 2		**36**
Alternative 3:		
Increase military spending to the highest of the options shown in Table 2-5 (from $75 billion to $92 billion)	−17	
Adopt the high option on farm programs shown in Table 4-15 (the Farm Coalition bill)	−1	
Fiscal dividend, Alternative 3		**−5**

Source: Authors' estimates.
a. All figures rounded to nearest billion.

the fiscal dividend, and they should be pursued. But in all realism, their yield is likely to be modest.

All of the alternative projections of the fiscal dividend assume no change in current tax laws, except for the revenues associated with an extension of existing automobile and telephone excises in the second alternative. But there is nothing inviolate about current tax laws. If as a nation we decide to use more than one-fifth of our income for federal programs, there is no economic or technical reason why we cannot do so. To raise the federal share of GNP from 20 to 21 percent, which would provide another $14 billion for public programs in 1975, would require only an act of political will in the form of a tax increase. Within the federal budget, the application of priority judgments requires that one public program be weighed against another. But we can, if we wish, make a different kind of priority decision by weighing private expenditures against public expenditures. Taxes are the device that allows us to carry out such a decision.

A final point should be noted regarding the concept of the fiscal dividend. In theory it represents the sums likely to become available to the federal government for discretionary application to high priority objectives. But there are literally hundreds of federal programs. Since 1962 alone, some 180 *new* federal programs have been established, and their expenditures in fiscal 1971 will amount to about $25 billion. Each of these programs has its own supporters, clientele, and lobbyists. For each one, evidence can be mobilized to support an expansion in program outlays. In making priority judgments about how the slim available funds should be spent, the President and the Congress are not acting in a vacuum. They are beset by countless claims, pressures, and appeals. To assume that the entire fiscal dividend, whatever its size, will be available solely for allocation among high priority needs is to ignore the slippage that will undoubtedly occur in the necessary process of negotiating with and satisfying at least some of these claimants. Hence, insofar as the fiscal dividend is interpreted as a sum available strictly for the most urgent public needs, the estimates presented above are surely on the high side.

Notes

Chapter 2: Defense

1. *The Budget of the United States Government, Fiscal Year 1971*, p. 84.
2. *United States Foreign Policy for the 1970's: A New Strategy for Peace*, Message from the President of the United States Transmitting a Report on Foreign Relations, H. Doc. 91–258, 91 Cong. 2 sess. (1970), p. 122.
3. *Statement of Secretary of Defense Melvin R. Laird before a Joint Session of the Senate Armed Services Committee and the Senate Subcommittee on Department of Defense Appropriations on the Fiscal Year 1971 Defense Program and Budget*, U.S. Department of Defense (Feb. 20, 1970), p. 53.
4. *U.S. Foreign Policy for the 1970's*, Message from the President, p. 129.
5. *Statement of Secretary of Defense Robert S. McNamara before the Senate Armed Services Committee on the Fiscal Year 1969–73 Defense Program and 1969 Defense Budget*, U.S. Department of Defense (Jan. 22, 1968), p. 81.
6. *Ibid.*, p. 85.
7. *Ibid.*, p. 126.
8. *Ibid.*, p. 82.
9. *Ibid.*, p. 83.
10. *Ibid.*, p. 82.
11. *Ibid.*, p. 84.
12. *Ibid.*, p. 79.
13. *Ibid.*, p. 139.
14. *Department of Defense Appropriations for 1969*, Hearings before a Subcommittee of the House Committee on Appropriations, 90 Cong. 2 sess. (1968). See the testimony of Robert S. McNamara, Feb. 14, 1968, Pt. 1, p. 93. According to an article in the *New York Times* of Jan. 17, 1969, a Cabinet Coordinating Committee on Economic Planning for the End of Vietnam Hostilities anticipated that if there were a truce in Vietnam, defense spending would decline by $19 billion in the following two and a half years.
15. Testimony of Robert C. Moot in *The Military Budget and National Economic Priorities*, Hearings before the Subcommittee on Economy in Government of the Joint Economic Committee, 91 Cong. 1 sess. (1969), Pt. 1, p. 307.

Chapter 3: Health, Education, and Income Maintenance

1. James E. Allen, Jr., "Preparing the Way for a New Era of Advancement in Education" (address to the convention of the American Association of School Administrators, Feb. 14, 1970; processed).

Chapter 4: Choices and Alternatives in Other Programs

1. *Economic Report of the President, February 1970*, p. 88. The small number of family formations in 1966 reflected the low birth rate during the depression and the Second World War.

2. The facts and observations about the new mass transit systems draw heavily on a paper by Martin Wohl, "The Nixon Transport Proposal" (Washington: Urban Institute, 1969; processed).

3. These paragraphs are derived from Walter W. Wilcox, "Economic Aspects of Farm Program Payment Limitations," Legislative Reference Service, Library of Congress, Nov. 6, 1969.

4. *The Post-Apollo Space Program: Directions for the Future*, Space Task Group Report to the President, September 1969, p. 20.

Chapter 5: Problems in Some Older Programs

1. Reported by Robert H. Haveman, *Water Resource Investment and the Public Interest: An Analysis of Federal Expenditures in Ten Southern States* (Vanderbilt University Press, 1965), Chap. 5.

2. Charles L. Schultze, *The Politics and Economics of Public Spending* (Brookings Institution, 1968), p. 90.

3. *Ibid.*, p. 91.

4. All data in this section are from U.S. Department of Health, Education, and Welfare, Office of Education, *Final Report on School Assistance in Federally Affected Areas: A Study of Public Laws 81–874 and 81–815* (prepared by Battelle Memorial Institute, December 1969).

TYPESETTING   *Monotype Composition Company, Inc., Baltimore*

PRINTING & BINDING   *Garamond/Pridemark Press, Inc., Baltimore*